**This book belongs to:**

..................................................

Mrs Wordsmith®

# THIRD GRADE ENGLISH

## SENSATIONAL WORKBOOK

# MEET THE
# CHARACTERS

Yang

Bogart

Oz

Yin

Armie

Shang
High

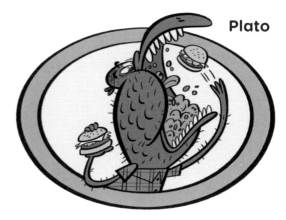

Bearnice

Brick

Grit

Plato

# CONTENTS

# Welcome to the 3rd Grade Sensational Workbook!

## What's inside?

In this book, you will find everything you need to blast through English in 3rd Grade. It is divided into six chapters: **Grammar**, **Punctuation**, **Vocabulary**, **Spelling**, **Reading and Writing**, and **Handwriting**. Each chapter combines targeted teaching of key skills, illustrations, and activities. It's perfect for those learning something for the first time and for those who are just studying!

## How do I use it?

However you want to! Start in the middle, start at the end, or even start at the beginning if you're feeling traditional. Take it slowly and do one section at a time, or charge through the pages like a gorilla on the loose! Don't worry if something is too difficult. You'll get there in the end, and there are tips and reminders to help you along the way.

Look out for this icon at the beginning of a new topic. It tells you that there's some important learning to do before you start answering the questions!

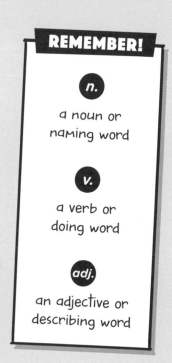

**REMEMBER!**

*n.*

a noun or naming word

*v.*

a verb or doing word

*adj.*

an adjective or describing word

## How do I check my answers?

There's an answer key at the back! Checking answers is an important part of learning. Take care to notice and remember the ones you didn't know.

Oh, and please excuse Mrs Wordsmith's cast of out-of-control animals. They pop up all over the place and are usually up to no good.

**Now, go and have some fun! And who knows, you might learn something along the way.**

# GRAMMAR

Grammar teaches you how to use different kinds of words (like verbs, nouns, or adjectives) and to form different kinds of sentences in the past, present, or future tense. When you master basic grammar rules, you have the power to talk or write about anything. When you master some more advanced grammar rules, you have the power to write beautifully.

A noun is the name of a **person** or **animal**, **place**, or **thing**. **Common nouns** name general places or things, for example:

**pizza**

**school**

**teacher**

**Proper nouns** name specific people, places, or things. These always begin with a capital letter, for example:

**Thailand**

**Bearnice**

**February**

**1** **Circle the common nouns and underline the proper nouns.**

**TIP!**
Nouns are sometimes called naming words.

| | | |
|---|---|---|
| book | dentist | <u>Grit</u> |
| (dog) | Nigeria | Cairo |
| tree | Wednesday | leg |
| city | blanket | December |

**2** **Now do the same with these sentences!**

Circle the common nouns and underline the proper nouns.

a. Yin and Yang danced in the kitchen.

b. Plato eats tacos every Tuesday.

c. The friends are flying to Germany in April.

A **phrase** is a group of words without a main verb.
A **noun phrase** is a group of words that tell you about a noun.

These can come in different lengths and styles, but they always add extra information about the noun.

**the smelly socks**

For example, both of these are noun phrases that describe **socks**:

**the smelly green socks with blue polka dots**

## 1 Circle the noun phrases.

Some of these are nouns and some are noun phrases.
Can you find the noun phrases?

the deep blue ocean

trampoline

the juggling ball

watermelon

a sour and juicy lemon

a chocolate chip cookie

## 2 Write your own!

Time to use your creativity! Rewrite these nouns as descriptive noun phrases.
The first one is done for you.

a. bed    the soft bed with plump pillows

b. school ........................................................

c. summer ........................................................

d. volcano ........................................................

e. mountain ........................................................

f. tiger ........................................................

# PRONOUNS

Pronouns are short words that can take the place of nouns in a sentence. Without pronouns, sentences can get repetitive very quickly.

**Plato** felt hungry. **Plato** opened the fridge
and **Plato** looked for something to eat.

Plato's name was mentioned
three times in that short story.

It's important to use Plato's name the
first time to introduce who the story is
about. After that, his name can be
replaced with pronouns.

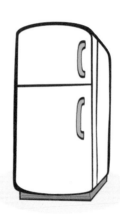

**Plato** felt hungry. **He** opened the fridge
and **he** looked for something to eat.

This makes the story less repetitive and easier to read!

| Pronoun | Who the pronoun refers to |
|---|---|
| I | yourself (the one reading this workbook!) |
| you | a person or group that you (the reader) are addressing |
| he | a male person |
| she | a female person |
| it | an object or thing |
| we | more than one person, including you (the reader) |
| they | more than one person, not including you (the reader) or a person whose gender you don't know or a person who does not identify as male or female |

**1 Rewrite these sentences and replace the nouns in bold with a suitable pronoun.**

Use the table on the opposite page to help you.

a. Brick loves onions and **Brick** has horrible breath.

.............................................................

.............................................................

b. The pizza is covered in green slime. **The pizza** is disgusting.

.............................................................

.............................................................

c. Yin and Yang are rowing across rough water. **Yin and Yang** are terrified.

.............................................................

.............................................................

d. Bearnice feels as though **Bearnice** has a thousand things to do.

.............................................................

Verbs are **doing** and **being** words. A **doing word** describes an action—for example, **climb** is a doing word. A **being word** describes a state of being—for example, **am** is a being word.

Brick **climbs** a tree.

I **am** happy.

**DID YOU KNOW?**

Whoever is doing the action or is in the state of being is also called the subject of the sentence.

The way a verb is written changes based on whoever is doing the action or is in the state of being. When the subject is **singular**, add **-s** to the verb.

He walk**s** home.

Bearnice jump**s** up.

When the subject is **plural** or the subject is **I** or **you**, do not add **-s** to the verb.

They walk home.

I jump up.

1 **Draw a line to match the subject to the verb.**

All of these subjects can either be paired with "run" or "runs" according to the rules above. Draw lines to match each pair.

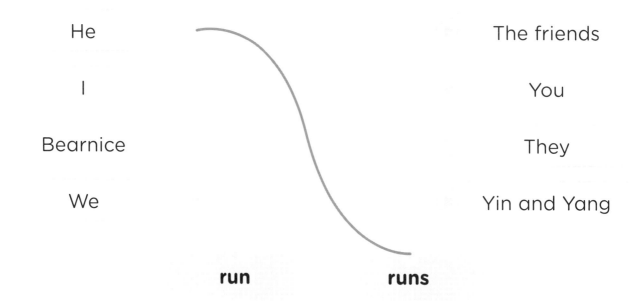

He

I

Bearnice

We

The friends

You

They

Yin and Yang

**run**　　　　　**runs**

## 2 Complete these sentences.

Circle the correct spelling.

a. Armie  **tiptoe**  **tiptoes**  through the silent library.

b. Shang High and Brick  **slide**  **slides**  quickly

down the snowy hill.

c. Yang  **love**  **loves**  her sister … most of the time.

d. Grit always  **forget**  **forgets**  to wash his socks.

e. Oz  **open**  **opens**  the golden treasure chest.

f. The twins  **change**  **changes**  their outfits five times

before leaving.

## 3 Now it's your turn!

Write your own sentences using as many of the verbs listed below
as possible. Remember to make sure your verbs make sense by leaving
off or adding the -**s**.

**explain(s)**     **collect(s)**     **order(s)**

**agree(s)**     **lose(s)**

a. ...........................................................................................................................

b. ...........................................................................................................................

c. ...........................................................................................................................

Tense tells us when something takes place. Things can happen in the past, present, or future. When a sentence has more than one verb in it, they are usually in the same tense.

The verbs in this sentence are in the present tense:

# Bearnice **plays** soccer and **scores** a goal.

The present tense can be used to talk about something that happens regularly.

**REMEMBER!**

When the subject is singular, add −s to the present tense verb. When the subject is plural or the subject is I or you, do not add −s to the present tense verb.

The verbs in this sentence are in the past tense:

# Bearnice **tripped** over her shoelaces and **landed** on the ground.

Remember, past tense verbs often end in -**ed**.

## 1 Rewrite these verbs in the past tense.
Tip! Watch out for your spellings.

a. adore ........................................

c. remember ........................................

b. touch ........................................

d. believe ........................................

## 2 Rewrite these verbs in the present tense.

Tip! Watch out for your spellings.

a. She wanted ...................................

b. I recognized ...................................

c. He imagined ...................................

d. You hated ...................................

## 3 Rewrite these sentences in the past tense.

a. Armie climbs to the top of the tallest mountain.

.............................................................

.............................................................

b. Grit aims his slingshot at a buzzing beehive.

.............................................................

.............................................................

c. Bearnice relaxes in an indulgent mud bath.

.............................................................

.............................................................

d. Shang High delivers pizza all around the world.

.............................................................

.............................................................

Regular past tense verbs end with -**ed**:

He **waved**.

However, irregular past tense verbs are
spelled and pronounced differently:

I **eat** lunch.  I **ate** lunch.

Irregular past tense words are ones that you have
to learn by heart, so let's get practicing!

## 1 Find the matching verbs.

Draw lines from the present tense verb to its
matching irregular past tense verb. It may look
a little different, but read through all the answers
to figure out which is which.

> **TIP!**
> It can be helpful to say
> the verbs aloud in a
> sentence, like "Today I
> sing" or "Yesterday I sang."

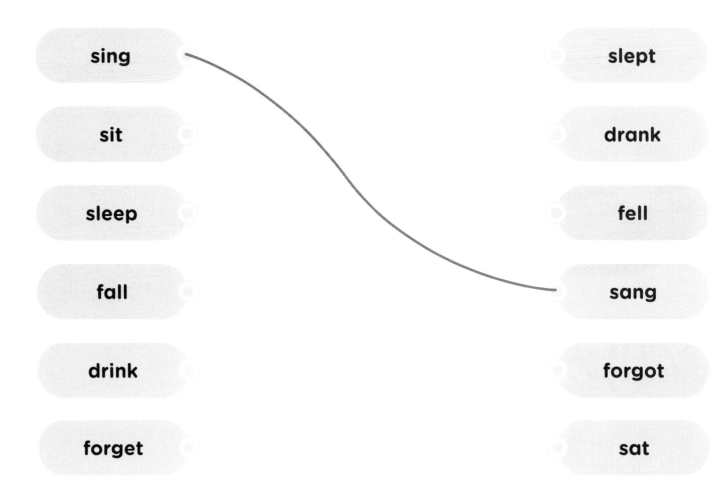

| | |
|---|---|
| sing | slept |
| sit | drank |
| sleep | fell |
| fall | sang |
| drink | forgot |
| forget | sat |

## 2  Rewrite these sentences in the past tense.

The verbs in bold are irregular in the past tense. You can use question 1 on the previous page to help you or test yourself by not looking!

a. Armie **sits** alone in the perfect spot to quietly read his favorite book.

..................................................

..................................................

..................................................

b. Plato **drinks** the juice from an extremely sour lemon.

..................................................

..................................................

..................................................

c. Brick **forgets** to check the measurements of his vacation home.

..................................................

..................................................

..................................................

d. Plato **sleeps** absolutely terribly.

..................................................

..................................................

Tense tells us when something takes place.
Things can happen in the past, present, or future.

When a sentence has more than
one verb in it, they are usually in
the same tense.

**1  Complete these sentences.**

Circle the correct form of the verb to keep the tense consistent.

a. Bearnice ran through the windy field and  loses
   lost  her umbrella.

b. Armie went to the library and  borrows  borrowed
   four books.

c. Yang shouts while she  chases  chased  the
   ice cream truck.

d. Plato licked his lips and  eats  ate  his famous
   strawberry and caramel pie.

e. Grit sniffs the ground and  follows  followed  the
   mysterious smell.

f. Shang High listened to music while he  walks  walked
   around the museum.

## 2 Edit Plato's diary.

Plato has made some mistakes in his diary. He forgot to stay in the same tense. Underline the verbs that are in the incorrect tense and write the correction below. Some of them are irregular past tense verbs, so make sure it sounds right when you read it aloud.

Dear Diary,

Yesterday, I went to the biggest theme park in the world.

It had 19 roller coasters and I ride 10 of them in one day!

My favorite was The Destructinator because it spun

around and makes me feel amazingly dizzy.

I have so much fun yesterday!

Plato

A and **an** are articles. They appear before nouns or noun phrases.

**A** loves consonant sounds!
**A** loves being close to consonant
sounds like **p** or **sh**.

# a pizza or a shop

**A** is very scared of vowel sounds
(**a**, **e**, **i**, **o**, and **u**). But **n** is a superhero!
**N** protects **a** from these scary vowels.

# an octopus or an egg

**1** **Complete these sentences with a or an.**

a. Oz dreams of becoming ................... actor.

b. Yin needed ................... key to unlock the secret door.

c. Grit sank into the soft cushions of ................... armchair.

d. Plato found ................... glove, three beans, and lots of

coins under his sofa.

e. Brick is going on vacation to ................... exotic island.

f. Bearnice slept in ................... igloo last night.

We use **a** or **an** when referring to general or nonspecific things.
We use **the** when talking about **specific** things.

**FOR EXAMPLE**

<u>**a**</u> bike

<u>**the**</u> bike

## 2 Complete these sentences.

Fill in the blanks with **a**, **an**, or **the**, choosing the article
that makes the most sense.

a. Plato can make ..................... delicious

dish out of any ingredients.

b. Yang loved mischief more than anything in ..................... world.

c. Bearnice made ..................... new snowball after her old one melted.

d. Oz was excited to visit ..................... Great Wall of China.

e. Grit's favorite snack was ..................... bowl of fresh bone stew.

f. Bearnice wore ..................... orange hat, ..................... purple scarf,

and ..................... green coat.

Most sentences are made up of clauses. A clause contains a verb.

A **main clause** forms a complete sentence on its own. This means that it doesn't need any extra information to make sense.

**Plato baked a pie.**

A **subordinate clause** does not make sense on its own. It adds extra information to the main clause and it contains a subordinating conjunction, such as **because**, **after**, **when**, or **until**.

Main
clause

Plato baked a pie
**because he was hungry.**

subordinate
clause

1 **Which type of clause are these?**

Draw a line from each clause to the correct label.

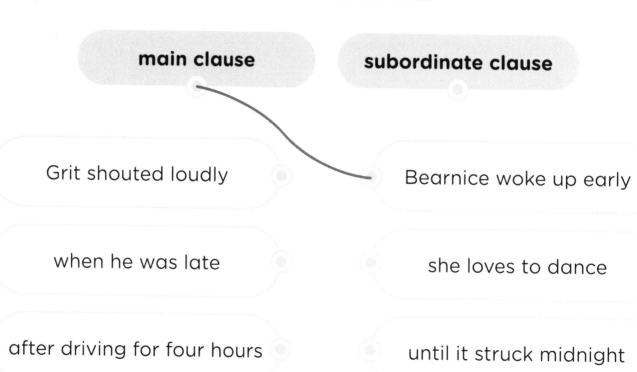

| main clause | subordinate clause |
|---|---|

Grit shouted loudly

Bearnice woke up early

when he was late

she loves to dance

after driving for four hours

until it struck midnight

Subordinate clauses can go at the end or the beginning of a sentence. When the subordinate clause is at the beginning, it is followed by a comma.

subordinate
clause

## I watched TV
## when I got home.

subordinating
conjunction

subordinate
clause

## When I got home,
## I watched TV.

main
clause

**2** **Complete these sentences.**

Draw a line to match the main clause to the subordinate clause to complete the sentences. Make sure they make sense!

| **main clause** | **subordinate clause** |
|---|---|
| a. Shang High was late to school | because it was too prickly. |
| b. Armie read his favorite book in bed | as she stepped onto the moon. |
| c. Bearnice felt out of breath | until he fell asleep. |
| d. The train broke down | after traveling for five minutes. |
| e. The astronaut held her breath | because he missed his bus. |
| f. No one wanted to touch the cactus | after being chased by a tiger. |

Conjunctions are joining words that connect
clauses (parts of a sentence).

The most common conjunctions are **and**, **or**, and **but**. They are
used to join two main clauses together. They are called coordinating
conjunctions. When we join two main clauses with a coordinating
conjunction, they form a compound sentence.

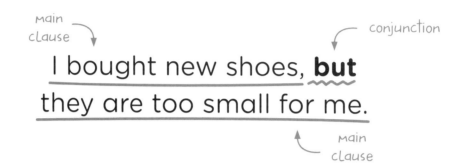

main
clause

conjunction

I bought new shoes, **but**
they are too small for me.

main
clause

### REMEMBER!

A main clause can form a complete sentence on its own,
but it can also form part of a compound sentence or complex sentence.

## 1 Underline the conjunction in these sentences

a. Grit doesn't like going outside
and he doesn't like meeting
new people.

b. There is an asteroid heading
for Earth, but the scientists
are not worried.

c. "Shall we play as pirates or
shall we play as mermaids?"
asked Yang.

d. Bogart plans to take over
the world and he won't let
anything stop him!

e. The corridor was dark,
but Armie slowly found
his way through.

f. Shang High needed a new
scarf, but he couldn't find one
long enough.

**2** **Add a conjunction to join these sentences.**

Rewrite each pair of sentences, using a conjunction to turn
them into one sentence.

| and | or | but |
|-----|-----|-----|

a. Yin was irritated with Yang. Yang was furious with Yin.

........................................................................................................

........................................................................................................

b. Bearnice knew Armie was thirsty. She refused to share her water.

........................................................................................................

........................................................................................................

c. Armie may be an inventor when he grows up.

He may be an engineer.

........................................................................................................

........................................................................................................

........................................................................................................

d. Oz is a beautiful singer. Grit is a talented pianist.

........................................................................................................

........................................................................................................

e. Shang High's room was a mess. He refused to clean it.

........................................................................................................

........................................................................................................

Conjunctions are joining words that connect two parts of a sentence. These parts are called clauses.

A **main clause** can form a complete sentence on its own, but it can also form part of a compound sentence or complex sentence.

A **subordinate clause** does not make sense on its own. It adds extra information to the main clause.

*main clause*

Plato's stomach grumbled **because** he smelled something delicious.

*subordinate clause*

*subordinate clause*

**When** she concentrates really hard, Oz can see into the future.

*main clause*

Some common subordinating conjunctions that link a subordinate clause to a main clause are:

| | |
|---|---|
| **because** | **so** |
| **when** | **as** |
| **after** | **until** |

**DID YOU KNOW?**

Subordinate clauses can go at the end or the beginning of a sentence. When the subordinate clause is at the beginning, it is followed by a comma.

Plato fell asleep **after** he ate all the pies.

*subordinating conjunction*

*subordinate clause*

**After he ate all the pies**, Plato fell asleep.

*main clause*

**1** **Underline the subordinating conjunction in these sentences.**
Remember, subordinate clauses sometimes go at the beginning of a sentence.

a. Brick lifts weights every day so he can get big and strong.

b. Yin and Yang hid under the desk until their teacher left the room.

c. Grit can play outside when it stops raining.

d. Bearnice loves bowling because she always wins.

e. After finishing his current book, Armie immediately started another one.

**2** **Now it's your turn!**
Write three sentences about your friends, including a subordinate clause and subordinating conjunction in each. Use the conjunctions below to help you.

> because    when    after
>
> so    until    as

a. My best friend loves to play ......................................

...................................................................................................

b. ...................................................................................................

...................................................................................................

c. ...................................................................................................

...................................................................................................

Adjectives are words that describe **nouns**. Remember,
a noun is the **name** of a **person** or **animal**, **place**, or **thing**.

**1** **Circle the adjectives.**

moldy      squeeze      rapid

brilliant      overpriced      sprint

**2** **Match the noun to the adjective that best describes it.**

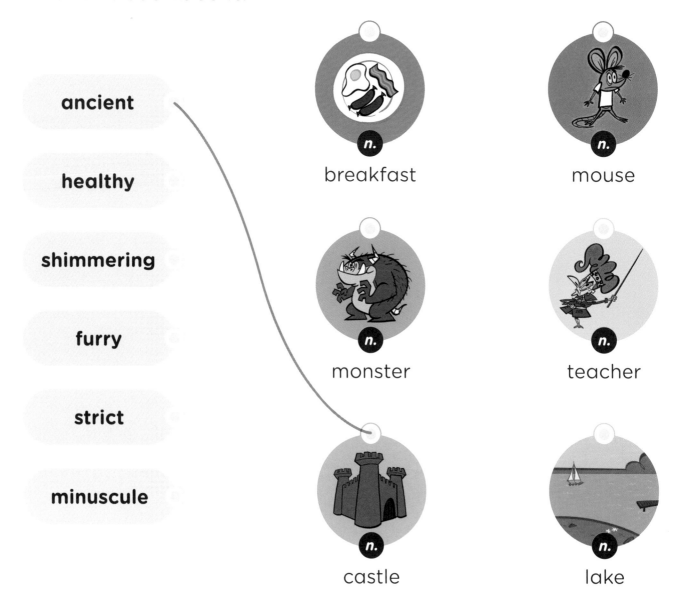

ancient

healthy

shimmering

furry

strict

minuscule

breakfast

mouse

monster

teacher

castle

lake

## 3 Complete these sentences.

Fill in the blanks with one of these adjectives or choose your own!

| | | | |
|---|---|---|---|
| disgusting | delicious | nauseating | colorful |
| chirping | vibrant | loud | delectable |

a. The ............................................................

sandwich made Shang High feel sick.

b. Bogart celebrated with

.......................................... confetti.

c. Brick dropped his

..........................................................

ice cream on the floor.

d. Grit couldn't sleep because of the

.......................................... birds.

Adverbs **describe verbs**. Remember,
a verb is a doing or being word.

Adverbs often end in **-ly**. They describe
how or when we do things.

**1** **Circle the adverbs.**

| angrily | wildly | blue |
|---------|--------|------|

| usually | daily | circular |
|---------|-------|----------|

**2** **Transform the underlined words into adverbs!**

Add the suffix **-ly** to complete the sentences. Read the sentences
aloud to help you. The first one is done for you!

a. Grit was <u>brave</u> as he fought.

Grit fought _____bravely_____ .

b. Yin was <u>nervous</u> as she sang.

Yin sang _____ .

c. Bearnice was <u>kind</u> as she spoke.

Bearnice spoke _____ .

## 3 Complete these sentences.

Fill in the blanks with one of these adverbs or choose
your own! The first one has been done for you.

| nervously | sometimes | angrily | cautiously |

a. Armie peered **nervously** .................. over the top of the diving board.

b. Bogart reached out

.......................................... .

c. .........................................., Yang is not very nice to her sister.

d. Grit quit his game .......................................... .

A phrase is a group of words without a verb. For example:

**wet and slimy**

**after breakfast**

**1** **Circle the phrases.**

The goose ran.

very quietly

yesterday afternoon

really happy

I am jumping up and down.

**2** **Complete these sentences with your own phrases.**

a. Armie read ................................................................................................. .

b. The waiter walked away .......................................................................... .

c. The ocean is .............................................................................................. .

d. Yin and Yang slept ................................................................................... .

Some phrases behave like adverbs. **Adverbial phrases** describe how, when, or where a verb happens.

Oz met Armie **by the popcorn stand**.

When these adverbial sentences go at the start of a sentence and add extra information, they are called **fronted adverbials**.

**This afternoon**, I learned all about phrases!

## 3 Complete these sentences.

Fill in the blanks using the options in the box.
Some adverbials might work in more than
one sentence, so choose the one you think
makes the most sense.

**TIP!**

Fronted adverbials are
always followed by a comma
that separates them from the
rest of the sentence.

| In the morning | Completely exhausted | Trembling with excitement |
| At the bottom of the sea | As soon as she could | Under the floorboards |

a. ................................................................ , Oz made

herself her famous, triple-stacked pancakes.

b. ................................................................ , the pirate

captain docked at the shore.

c. ................................................................ , the explorer

placed the key into the chest.

d. ................................................................ , she locked the

back door and bolted the windows.

e. ................................................................ , a giant

octopus was sleeping peacefully.

f. ................................................................ , thousands of

mice were forming a plan.

A sentence is a complete idea that makes sense by itself.
There are four different types of complete sentences:
statements, questions, commands, and exclamation sentences.

A **statement** expresses a fact, idea, or opinion.
This is the most common type of sentence.
It usually ends with a period, and the person
or thing doing the action comes before the verb:

# Armie is happy.

verb

A **question** asks something that needs an answer.
It always ends with a question mark. You can often turn
a statement into a question by putting the verb before
the person or thing that is doing the action.

# Is Armie happy?

verb

A **command** tells someone to do something.
It can end with a period or exclamation mark.

# Armie, be happy!

An **exclamation** sentence tells something with surprise
or strong feeling. It always ends with an exclamation mark.
Exclamation sentences start with "what" or "how."

# How happy Armie is!

**1** **Draw a line to match the sentence to their correct sentence types.**

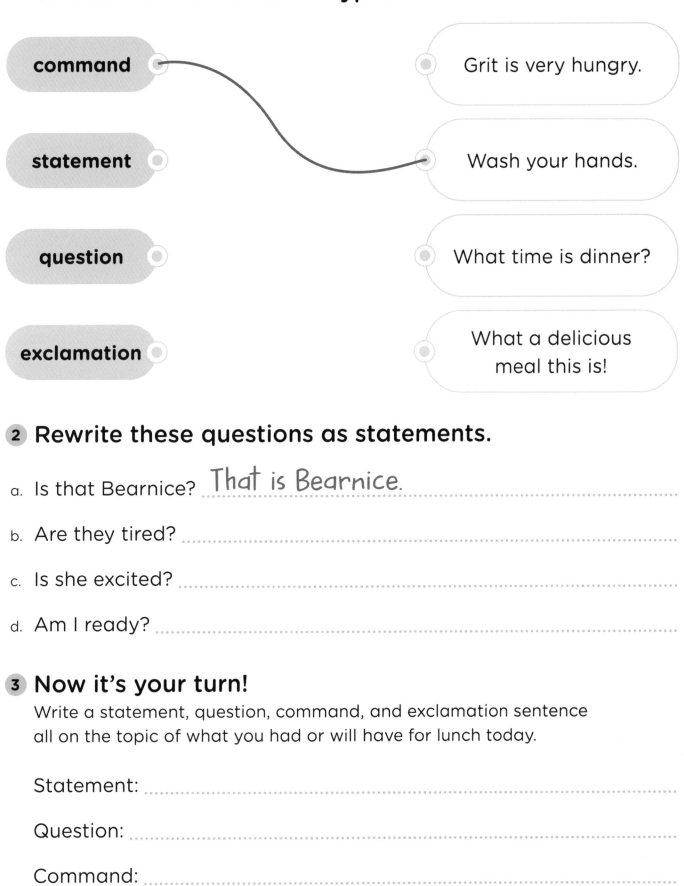

| command | | Grit is very hungry. |
| statement | | Wash your hands. |
| question | | What time is dinner? |
| exclamation | | What a delicious meal this is! |

**2** **Rewrite these questions as statements.**

a. Is that Bearnice? $\quad$ That is Bearnice. ................................

b. Are they tired? ................................................

c. Is she excited? ................................................

d. Am I ready? ................................................

**3** **Now it's your turn!**
Write a statement, question, command, and exclamation sentence all on the topic of what you had or will have for lunch today.

Statement: ................................................

Question: ................................................

Command: ................................................

Exclamation: ................................................

# PUNCTUATION

When we talk, we use the tone of our voices
to make our meaning clear. When we write,
we rely on punctuation instead. In this chapter,
you'll practice some key punctuation skills.

Apostrophes can be used to show contractions or possession.

Sometimes, apostrophes can show where letters
are missing in shortened versions of words.

These shortened versions of words are called contractions.

**Do not** worry, **you will**
love contractions!

**Don't** worry, **you'll**
love contractions!

**TIP!**

Sometimes, the contraction does not exactly match the words that it is made from—
for example, will not = won't.

**1** **Draw lines to match the words to their contractions.**

| | | | |
|---|---|---|---|
| a. | was not | | didn't |
| b. | we are | | I'm |
| c. | did not | | shouldn't |
| d. | should not | | we're |
| e. | you will | | won't |
| f. | I am | | wasn't |
| g. | she is | | you'll |
| h. | will not | | she's |

## 2 Rewrite these sentences with the correct contraction.

a. Plato **should not** have eaten Brick's lunch.

...................................................................................................................

b. **I am** very lost!

...................................................................................................................

c. The chef **will not** be making dessert.

...................................................................................................................

d. Bearnice **was not** alone in the haunted house.

...................................................................................................................

e. "I **did not** do that," lied Yang.

...................................................................................................................

f. **You will** love the lemon meringue pie!

...................................................................................................................

g. "**We are** twins!" said Yin and Yang.

...................................................................................................................

h. **She is** the first astronaut on Mars.

...................................................................................................................

Apostrophes can be used to show contractions or possession.

You can show that something belongs to someone (or something) by using an **apostrophe** and an **-s**.

There are four rules about how you can do this.

**1**

You may remember that for most **singular nouns**, we add an **apostrophe** and an **-s**.

**Plato's** food
is delicious.

**2**

It's trickier when **singular nouns end in -s**. In these cases, we add an **apostrophe only**.

**Thomas'** backpack
is blue.

**1** **Complete these possessive apostrophe equations.**
Add **an apostrophe and an s** or **an apostrophe only** to each noun.

a. Plato + spoon        ➡        Plato's spoon
.............................................

b. James + garden       ➡
.............................................

c. Armie + pencil       ➡
.............................................

d. Bearnice + pillow    ➡
.............................................

e. Chris + phone        ➡
.............................................

f. Bogart + plan        ➡
.............................................

**3**

When a noun has a **regular plural** (ending in -**s**) to show belonging, you add an **apostrophe only**.

The **elephants'** trunks are very long.

**4**

However, some **irregular plural nouns** (like one child, many children) do not end in -**s**. Here, you add an **apostrophe** and an -**s**.

The **children's** lunch is cold.

## 2 Rewrite these sentences as phrases.

Use an apostrophe to show belonging.

a. This water belongs to the teachers.

The teachers' water

b. This desk belongs to the school.

................................................................................................

c. The plants belong to the women.

................................................................................................

d. The coat belongs to Tobias.

................................................................................................

e. The potatoes belong to the chef.

................................................................................................

f. The weights belong to Brick.

................................................................................................

................................................................................................

Its is an exception and doesn't follow the same rules.
It's and its look similar but mean very different things.

It's is a contraction meaning it is or it has.

## It's nice to meet you.
## It's been raining all afternoon.

Its means belonging to it. It is an exception because
it doesn't have an apostrophe.

## This car has a scratch on its window.

## ① Circle the correct spelling of it's or its.

If you aren't sure, try reading the sentence out loud
using it is or it has to see if it makes sense.

a.  "    **It's**         **Its**         impossible!" cried Bogart.

b.  Never judge a book by    **it's**        **its**        cover.

c.  The plant grew too large for    **it's**        **its**    pot.

d.  **It's**        **Its**        been an unforgettable day!

## ② Rewrite these sentences.

Expand the contraction it's to it is or it has, using the rest of the sentence
(the context) to work out which makes the most sense.

a.  It's been a long day.

..............................................................................................................

b.  "It's only a ten-minute walk," she promised.

..............................................................................................................

You're and **your** look similar and sound the same but mean very different things.

**You're** is a contraction of **you are**.

**You're** holding my cactus.

**Your** means belonging to you.

I am holding **your** cactus.

**1** **Complete these sentences with you're or your.**

Read it aloud with the expanded form of the contraction to see which makes sense.

a. Where is ........................... new bike?

b. Always try ........................... best.

c. "Let me know when ........................... ready," said Oz.

d. ........................... an amazing person!

e. Please insert ........................... password.

f. "I'm so happy ........................... here!" cried Plato.

g. "Is this ........................... house?" asked Bearnice.

h. "Let me know when ........................... in town!" replied Yin.

There are three times when you need to remember to use capital letters:

at the **start** of each **sentence**

when writing names of **people**, **places**, **the days of the week**, and **months**—these are called **proper nouns**

when writing **I**

**A**fter lunch on **S**unday, **P**lato and **I** took a long nap.

**REMEMBER!**

Sentences always start with a capital letter and usually end with a period.

**1** **Circle the proper nouns that should start with a capital letter.**

april

pineapple

bogart

tokyo

climbing

**2** **Correct these sentences.**

Circle the letters that should be capitalized and add periods to the end of sentences.

a. it all began on a dark and stormy night in december

b. yin and yang go bowling every tuesday

c. "bogart and i have a cunning plan," admitted brick

d. plato dreams of opening a restaurant in thailand

## 3 Rewrite these sentences with the correct capitalization.

Don't forget to also add periods at the end of the sentences.

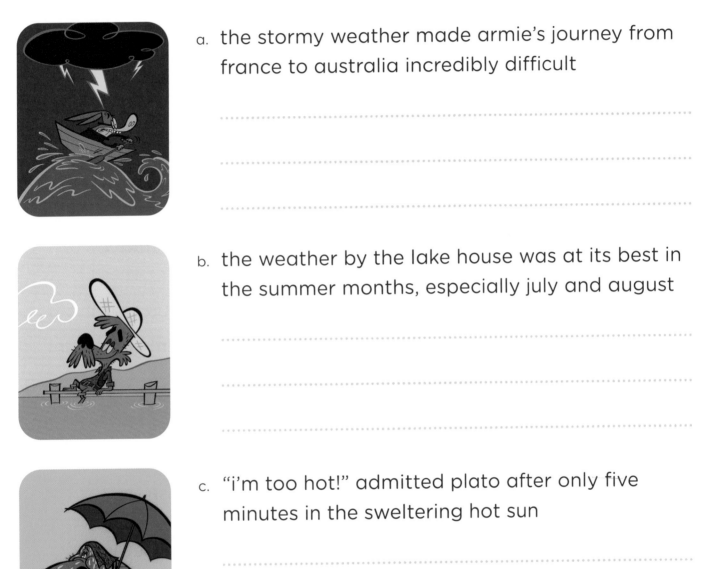

a. the stormy weather made armie's journey from france to australia incredibly difficult

...................................................

...................................................

...................................................

b. the weather by the lake house was at its best in the summer months, especially july and august

...................................................

...................................................

...................................................

c. "i'm too hot!" admitted plato after only five minutes in the sweltering hot sun

...................................................

...................................................

...................................................

d. brick realized that he hadn't showered since monday ... four weeks ago

...................................................

...................................................

A **question** asks something that needs an answer.
It always ends with a question mark.

Questions sometimes start with question words,
including **who**, **what**, **when**, **where**, **why**, and **how**.

## 1 Complete these sentences with punctuation.

Read the following sentences to decide whether they need a period
or a question mark.

a. What time are we leaving

b. The forest is full of wildlife

c. Have you seen my
sparkly socks

d. Why do triangles have
three sides

e. This is a delicious carrot

f. Are you eating my croissant

## 2 Match these sentence parts.

Draw lines to match the parts of a sentence to form a complete question.

| | |
|---|---|
| How does | my left shoe? |
| Where is | the internet work? |
| When are | the sky blue? |
| Why is | we going to school? |

## 3 Now it's your turn!

Write a question about the following topics. Don't forget to start with a
question word and end with a question mark.

a. Age: ................................................................................................................

b. Jellyfish: ........................................................................................................

An **exclamation** sentence tells something with surprise
or with strong feeling. It always ends with an exclamation mark.
Exclamation sentences start with **what** or **how**.

**Exclamation marks** can be used to show strong feelings.
They can be used at the end of a statement,
a command, or an exclamation sentence.

There's a shark in the water**!**
Get out of the water**!**
How lucky we were that we spotted it**!**

An exclamation mark can also show that something is said loudly.

"No**!**" screamed Brick.

## 1 Which sentences would you choose to give an exclamation mark?

Decide whether these sentences should end in a period, question mark, or exclamation mark. Read them aloud to work out how they are said.

a. He is seven years old

b. Stop that

c. Yang likes to paint

d. We won

e. What time is it

f. There's a fire

## 2 Now it's your turn!

Write a sentence ending with an exclamation mark to match the picture.

.......................................................

.......................................................

.......................................................

**Inverted commas** are used to show that someone is speaking.

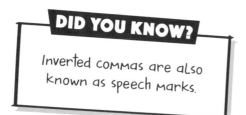

**DID YOU KNOW?**

Inverted commas are also known as speech marks.

Inverted commas go at the **start** and **end** of speech.

When the speech goes first in the sentence,
there is a punctuation mark before the final inverted comma.

**①**

If it's a **statement**, use a **comma**.

"I'm going to the park**,**" said Plato.

**②**

If it's a **question**, use a **question mark**.

"What time is it**?**" asked Oz.

**③**

If it's an **exclamation sentence**, has a strong feeling,
or is said loudly, use an **exclamation mark**.

"How exciting that is**!**" squealed Bearnice.

**REMEMBER!**

The first word in a speech
sentence always starts
with a capital letter.

**1** **Fix these sentences by adding inverted commas.**

a. I'd like to borrow this book please, said Armie.

b. That bee stung me! cried Grit.

c. Why are carrots orange? wondered Bearnice.

d. Now mix together all the ingredients, instructed Oz.

**2** **Correct and rewrite these sentences.**
Don't forget to include inverted commas, punctuation marks, and capitalization.

a. thank you said plato

.....................................................................................................................

b. where are you going asked oz

.....................................................................................................................

c. stop that thief shouted bogart

.....................................................................................................................

d. see you tomorrow said yang

.....................................................................................................................

> **Commas** help the reader. They can be used to separate items in a list. You need a comma between all the items.
> Put **and** or **or** before the last item.
>
> Brick's favorite colors are red**,** orange**,** blue, **and** green.

## 1 Fix these sentences.

Add commas in the correct places.

a. Yin plays tennis on Mondays Thursdays and Fridays.

b. I can speak German Hindi Welsh Vietnamese and English.

c. Plato's favorite foods are tacos burritos burgers and noodles.

d. Oz has traveled to Switzerland Australia India and Brazil.

e. The days of the week are Monday Tuesday Wednesday Thursday Friday Saturday and Sunday.

## 2 Now it's your turn!

Write a simple shopping list of items that Grit might need to make a fruit salad. Remember to write this as a full sentence.

...........................................................................................................................................

...........................................................................................................................................

...........................................................................................................................................

...........................................................................................................................................

...........................................................................................................................................

...........................................................................................................................................

Sometimes, an item in a list can be more than one word, for example:

I am going to buy **a loaf of bread**,
**some strawberry yogurt**, and **a bubbly drink**.

You still need a comma between all the items.

### 3 Fix these sentences.

Add commas in the correct places, remembering to watch out for items that are more than one word!

a. Plato's favorite flavors are strawberry ripple cookie dough and chocolate chip.

b. Bearnice asked for a new laptop green sneakers and a birthday cake.

c. Grit helped clean the living room dust the shelves and wash the dishes.

d. Oz tasted the raspberry cupcake the cinnamon swirl the jelly doughnut and the hazelnut macaron.

Paragraphs make your writing easier to read by grouping together ideas in sections.

In narrative writing, paragraphs can be used to group ideas according to **time**, **person**, or **place**.

**REMEMBER!**

New paragraphs always start on a new line.

Let's have a look at two paragraphs from the same fiction text. Using your knowledge about paragraphs, describe out loud why the paragraphs change when they do:

Plato loves to cook every night of the week. He has mastered dishes from all over the world. Plato hopes to work as a chef in a restaurant one day.

Bearnice, on the other hand, is not as good at cooking. She has never made it beyond the basics. Once, she tried to boil an egg and ended up burning the egg, which is very difficult to do!

# 1 True or false?

The following statements are all about paragraphs. Check the statements that are true.

a. Paragraphs are used to group similar ideas. ◯

b. Paragraphs make writing more difficult to read. ◯

c. A new paragraph starts on the same line as the previous paragraph. ◯

d. Paragraphs make writing easier to read. ◯

# 2 Add the paragraph breaks.

In fiction (or narrative writing), it can be more difficult to remember when to start a new paragraph. You might start a new paragraph when you have a jump in time or place.

When we edit, we add // to show when a new paragraph should begin. Here is the beginning of a fiction story in which three paragraphs have been squashed together. Read the text and decide where each new paragraph should begin. The first one has been done for you.

Once upon a time, there was a troll named Steve who loved to dance. He loved to dance so much that his feet didn't even stop moving when he was asleep. He danced the tango and he danced the waltz. He danced ballet and he danced street dance. He danced dances that didn't even have names yet.//This troll lived under a bridge in a faraway land named Trollbridge. Trollbridge was a town that consisted entirely of bridges. Under every bridge, there lived a troll. It was a quiet, peaceful place. The other trolls did not understand Steve's constant dancing. Dancing was not something that trolls did and because of this, many of the other trolls made fun of Steve for his rhythmic feet.

In nonfiction writing, paragraphs are often organized by **topic**. A topic can be anything from Australia, to frogs, to a sports game. Let's have a look at two paragraphs from the same nonfiction text. Using your knowledge about paragraphs, describe out loud why the paragraphs change when they do:

In the first half of the game, the blue team played well together. They passed the ball to each other constantly and managed to get around the red team enough times to score three spectacular points. The crowd went wild.

Unfortunately, the second half of the game did not go quite as planned. Four blue team players crashed into each other, another blue team player completely forgot the rules, and to top it all off, it started raining heavily. In the end, the blue team lost.

**1  Which sentences could be in the same paragraph?**

Draw lines to match sentences that are about the same **person**, **topic**, or **time**.

a.  Snakes are reptiles.

The capital city is Kuala Lumpur, and the official language is Malay.

b.  Thursday will feature heavy showers.

Jewelry can be very expensive.

c.  The stolen necklace was made of diamonds.

Other reptiles include crocodiles and turtles.

d.  Malaysia is a country in southeast Asia.

Things will start to brighten up on Friday.

## 2 Where are the two missing paragraph breaks?

This text has been written without paragraphs. Draw lines (like this //) in two places where you think a paragraph should end and a new one should begin.

Planet Earth is the fifth largest planet in our solar system. It is the only planet that is not named after Greek and Roman gods or goddesses. Planet Earth has one moon. Jupiter is the largest planet in the solar system. It spins faster than all the other planets. Scientists think that Jupiter has 79 moons. Mercury is the closest planet to the sun and one of the closest planets to Earth. It is also the smallest planet in our solar system. Mercury does not have any moons.

**TIP!**

Read the whole text before you decide where the paragraphs should go!

## 3 Now it's your turn!

Write two short paragraphs (at least three sentences each) on any of the following topics:

**your family**     **your school**     **your vacation**     **your friends**

Headings and subheadings are titles that tell the reader about the text.

A **heading** tells the reader about the **main topic** of the text.
If the text is split up into smaller sections, these may have
**subheadings** to tell the reader what the **smaller section** is about.

These different types of titles make the text clearer and easier to read.

**DID YOU KNOW?**

Headings and subheadings
are usually found in nonfiction texts.

**1 Match the paragraph to the subheading.**

The heading of these paragraphs is **Water**. Draw lines to label each
paragraph with a suitable subheading.

## WATER

**Puddles**        **Oceans**       **Rivers**

| | | |
|---|---|---|
| Large natural streams of water flow through land toward the sea. One of the most famous is the Nile River in northeastern Africa. | Huge expanses of saltwater cover most of the Earth's surface. Some examples include the Atlantic, Pacific, Indian, and Arctic Ocean. | Small pools of water collect on the ground after it rains. They are especially fun to jump in while wearing rain boots! |

## 2 What subheadings would you give each of these paragraphs?

These paragraphs are from a longer text called "**Our Solar System**."
Choose a suitable subheading for each one.

a. ......................................................................................................................................

Mars is over 239 million miles (385 million kilometers) from Earth. It is sometimes called the Red Planet because the soil looks like rusty iron. Mars has the largest dust storms in the solar system, and two small moons named Phobos and Deimos.

b. ......................................................................................................................................

The sun is a star at the center of our solar system. This means that all objects in our solar system orbit around the sun. It is over 4.5 billion years old and its surface temperature is about 9,941 degrees Fahrenheit (5,505 degrees Celsius). That's about 300 times hotter than the average temperature on Earth!

c. ......................................................................................................................................

There are 181 moons in the solar system. A moon is a large, natural object that orbits a planet. Moons do not emit their own light, but they can reflect the light of the sun. It takes 27.3 days for the Earth's moon to complete an orbit around Earth.

# VOCABULARY

Vocabulary is probably the most important part of learning to read and write. You wouldn't be able to read this sentence if you didn't know what all the words meant! Knowing lots of synonyms and their various shades of meaning helps you express yourself more accurately. Learning about prefixes and suffixes gives you clues about what new words mean when you come across them.

## HAPPY WORDS

## SAD WORDS

| | | | |
|---|---|---|---|
| delighted | contented | gloomy | glum |
| overjoyed | jubilant | sorrowful | miserable |
| ecstatic | thrilled | somber | melancholy |

## ① Find the synonyms.

There are lots of words that mean the same thing as happy or sad. Underline the two synonyms for happy or sad in each sentence. The first one has been done for you.

**REMEMBER!**

A synonym is a word that means the same or nearly the same as another word.

a. Armie discovered the secret to being happy. He repeated "I'm ecstatic!" ten times in the mirror.

b. Shang High felt sad that he was too tall to ride the rollercoaster. He'd never been so glum before.

c. Plato was miserable when his restaurant closed down. He felt melancholy as he locked the door for the last time.

d. Yin biked to school, delighted with her new bicycle. She was very thrilled about the rocket booster on the back wheel.

e. Bogart's sorrowful eyes filled with tears. He always felt particularly gloomy when his plans to take over the world failed.

## 2 Upgrade these sentences.

Cross out the word happy or sad and replace it with a synonym. The first one has been done for you.

glum
a. Plato felt ~~sad~~ when he dropped his triple chocolate ice cream.

b. When Grit was a happy dog, he wagged his tail.

c. "Noooo!" cried Oz as her laboratory exploded. It was a sad day.

d. "I'm happy to be here," lied Brick through gritted teeth.

e. Bogart loves to read sad books. His favorite is about a lonely worm who has no friends.

f. Yin hugged Yang tightly. She was happy to be reunited with her sister.

# 1 Match these word pairs to the right senses!

Which part of your body do you use to sense these things? Using the key on the opposite page, write the correct number under each picture.

a.
**reeking** sewer

⑤

b.
**pungent** sock

c.
**juicy** burger

d.
**slimy** scales

e.
**shrill** whistle

f.
**peppery** hot sauce

g.
**blaring** siren

h.
**stinking** dung

i.
**colorful** painting

j.
**spicy** taco

k.
**thunderous** drums

l.
**pretty** landscape

m. **tart** lemonade

n. **soft** fur

o. **loud** trumpet

p. **beautiful** orchard

q. **stinging** nettles

r. **comfy** pillow

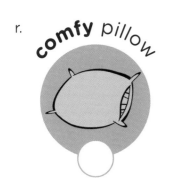

s. **scented** candle

t. **sparkling** lagoon

**KEY**

1 **touch**

2 **taste**

3 **hearing**

4 **sight**

5 **smell**

**Compound words** are made of two words that are joined together to make one word, like popcorn.

**pop** ✛ **corn** ═ **popcorn**

**1** Combine these images to form a compound word.

a.

 ✛  ═

........................................................

b.

 ✛  ═

........................................................

c.

 ✛  ═

........................................................

d.

 ✛  ═

........................................................

e.

 ✛  ═

........................................................

## 2 Make compound words and write sentences!

Find words that combine into compound words. Use these compound words to write five different sentences. The first one is done for you.

| | | | | |
|---|---|---|---|---|
| foot | after | cow | pan | boy |
| moon | cake | noon | light | ball |

a. My sentence using: moonlight

The moonlight sparkled on the surface of the lake.

b. My sentence using:

c. My sentence using:

d. My sentence using:

e. My sentence using:

Some words are made up of different parts. The main part is called the **root word**. The root word carries the meaning.

A root word is a real word. **Prefixes** and **suffixes** (a letter or a group of letters) can be added to the root word to alter the meaning. Sometimes, we have to adjust the spelling when we add a suffix.

If you add the prefix **un**- to the beginning of the root word **happy**, you make a new word:

prefix un–        **un**happy        Root word

If you add a suffix like -**ness** or -**ly** to the end of the root word **happy**, you make a different word:

Root word        happi**ness**        suffix –ness

happi**ly**        suffix –ly
Root word

**Unhappy**, **happiness**, and **happily**
are all made using the same root word.
The spellings and meanings of these words are related.

Happy, unhappy, happiness, and happily all belong to the same **word family**.

**TIP!**

When we notice things like root words, it helps develop our word consciousness. This is our awareness of words that helps us spell and learn new vocabulary.

# 1 Connect the word families that share a root word!

Draw a line from words in the first column to words in the other columns from the same word family. The first one is done for you.

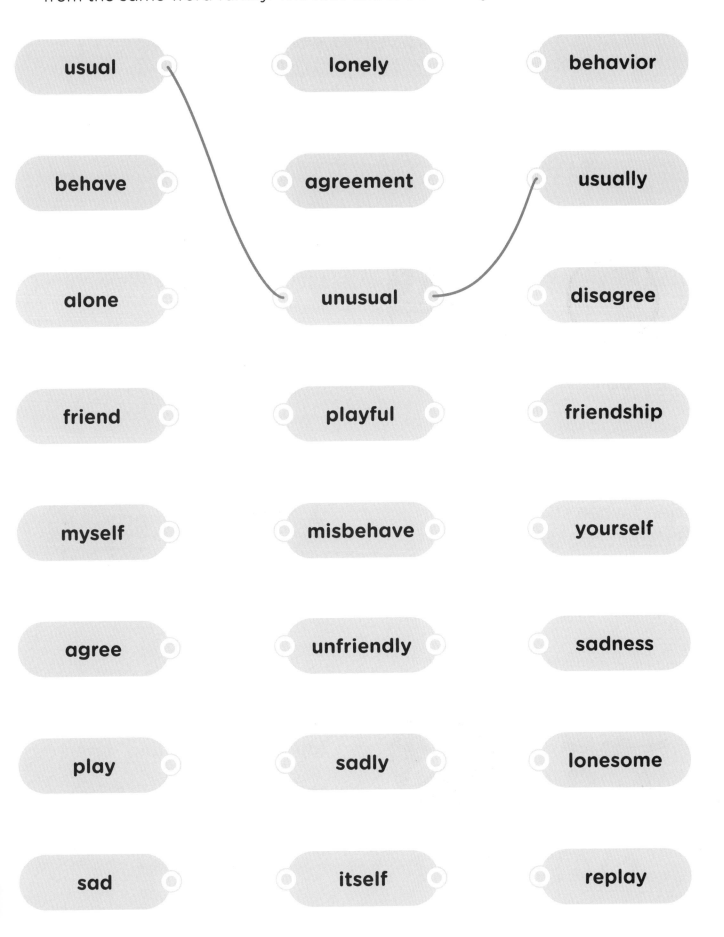

| usual | lonely | behavior |
| behave | agreement | usually |
| alone | unusual | disagree |
| friend | playful | friendship |
| myself | misbehave | yourself |
| agree | unfriendly | sadness |
| play | sadly | lonesome |
| sad | itself | replay |

Homophones are words that **sound the same** but are **spelled differently** and have **different meanings**.

This page introduces lots of different homophones. Read through them and try to remember as many as you can because they will help you complete the next few activities. If you need some help later on, you can look back to this page for a reminder!

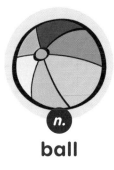

*n.*
**ball**

*v.*
**bawl**

**weather**—Always carry an umbrella because the weather is unpredictable.

**whether**—I'm going to the party whether you like it or not!

**missed**—I really missed my friend when she moved to a different country.

**mist**—We couldn't see a thing through the dense mist.

*n.*
**rain**

*n.*
**reign**

*n.*
**knot**

*adv.*
**not**

**fair**—"That's not fair!" cried Oz.

**fare**—The bus fare is $2.50.

**berry** — *n.*

**bury** — *v.*

**grate**—Plato loves to grate a lot of cheese onto his pasta.

**great**—Have you heard the great news?

**main**—They drove for hours down the main road.

**mane**—The lion had a beautiful golden mane.

**meat** — *n.*

**meet** — *v.*

**cymbal** — *n.*

**symbol** — *n.*

**medal**—The athlete won his fourteenth gold medal.

**meddle**—The prankster loved to meddle with people's lives.

**ate**—I crept out of bed and ate a midnight snack

**eight**—The alarm went off at eight o'clock sharp.

**hair** — *n.*

**hare** — *n.*

## 1 Match the homophones to the pictures!

The words below are homophones. This means that they sound the same but are spelled differently and have different meanings. Draw a line connecting each word to the right picture.

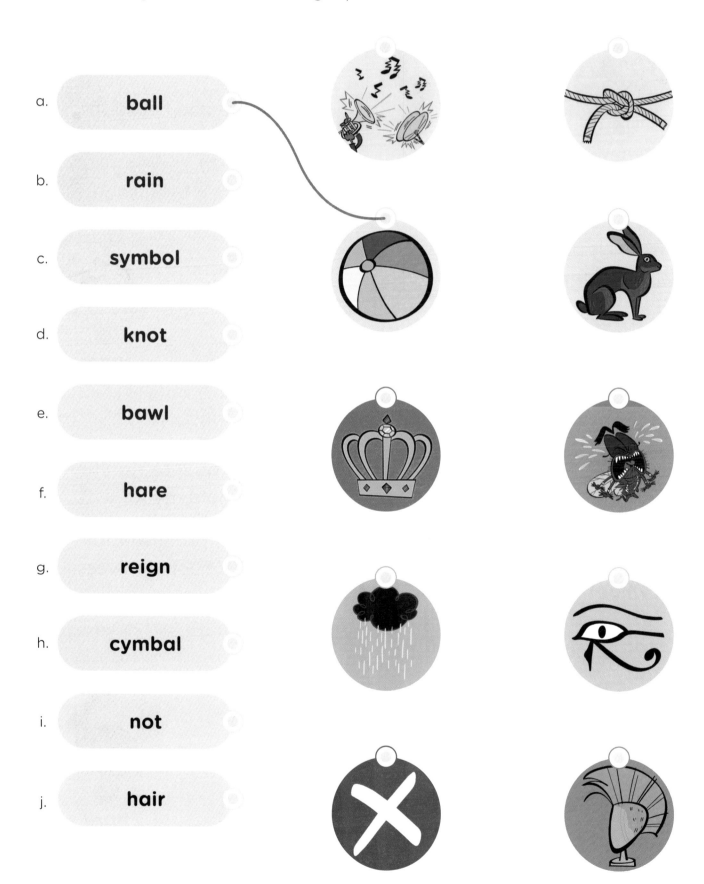

a. ball

b. rain

c. symbol

d. knot

e. bawl

f. hare

g. reign

h. cymbal

i. not

j. hair

## 2 Complete these common phrases.

The phrases below are missing a word. Can you figure out which one
goes with **rain** and which one goes with **reign**? Draw a line connecting
each word to the right picture.

rain

reign

a. The King's brief ...

b. ... fall

c. The Queen's lengthy ...

d. The BBQ was ruined by ...

e. The ... turned into snow

f. It's pouring ...

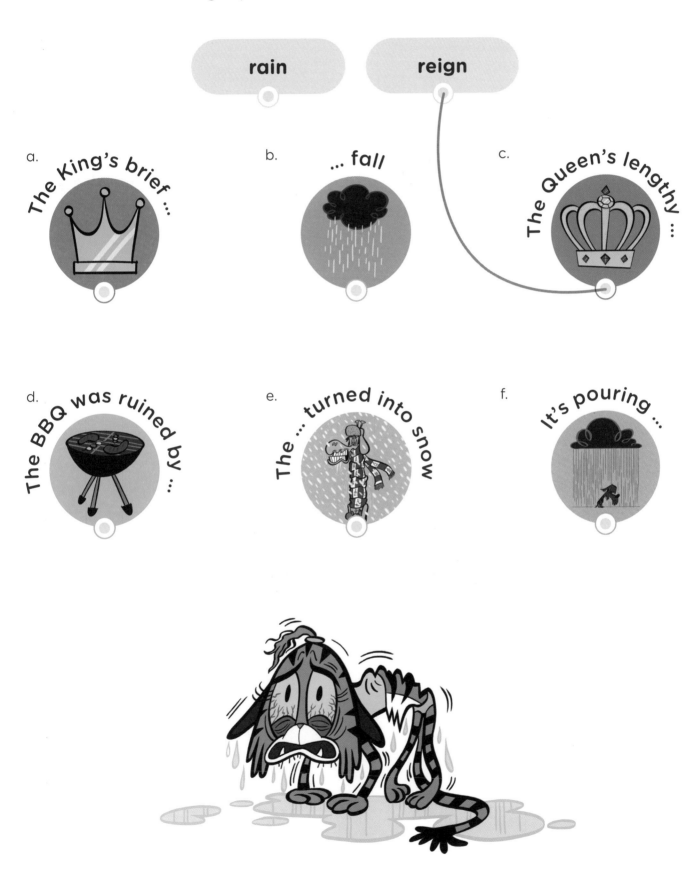

## ③ Circle the homophone that matches the picture.

The words below are homophones. This means that they sound the same but are spelled differently and have different meanings.

a.

**meat**

**meet**

b.

**weather**

**whether**

c.

**berry**

**bury**

d.

**fair**

**fare**

e.

**grate**

**great**

f.

**main**

**mane**

g.

**medal**

**meddle**

h.

**missed**

**mist**

# 4 Complete the sentences with the correct word.

Choose the correct spelling and fill in the blanks.

a. Grit counted ........................................ other

buses before his bus arrived!

ate        eight

b. "What a ........................................ day,"

said Brick with a contented smile.

grate        great

c. The pirate decided to ........................................

the treasure in a hole in his yard.

berry        bury

d. Plato was undecided about

........................................ to have a sandwich

or tacos for lunch.

weather        whether

e. "I've always wanted to ........................................

you!" squealed Oz.

meat        meet

Multiple-meaning words are words that have the same spelling and usually sound alike but have different meanings.

## Bearnice **left** through the door on the **left**.

Here, Left means to exit or Leave

Here, Left means the opposite of right

## 1 Spot the multiple-meaning words.

Read these sentences and circle the multiple-meaning words. Describe out loud the two different meanings.

a. The pirate felt his heart beating in his chest as he nervously placed the key into the locked treasure chest.

b. When the bathroom tap stopped working, the plumber fixed it by giving the pipes a gentle tap with a hammer.

c. Yang loves to lie in bed all day, then lie to Yin about the adventures she went on that day.

d. "Ouch! My foot!" cried the astonished swimmer as she stubbed her toe on the pool floor. She had not realized the water was only 1 foot deep.

## 2 Match the sentences to the correct images.

These sentences contain homonyms. Draw lines to match each sentence to the correct image.

a. Plato hit the nails with a hammer.

b. Oz painted her nails bright purple.

c. In the future, cars will be able to fly.

d. Bogart is a cunning fly.

e. You need a stamp to mail a letter.

f. Brick tried to stamp on Bogart!

A synonym is a word that means the same
or nearly the same as another word.

Some words have similar meanings,
but one is stronger than the other.

Brick **dislikes**
mushrooms.

Plato **loathes**
mushrooms.

The words **dislike** and **loathe** both have a similar meaning to
the word **hate**, but you might use loathe when you are talking
about something you **really really hate**.

**Inedible** is more
disgusting than **gross**.

**Flabbergasted** is more
shocked than **startled**.

**Putrid** is more smelly
than **stinking**.

# ① Which sentence uses the strongest synonym?

Read the sentences and answer the questions. These synonyms may have the same or similar meanings, but one is stronger than the other.

a. Shang High's socks are stinking. Brick's socks are putrid.

Whose socks are the smelliest?

.......................................................................................................................................

b. Oz is startled by the news. Yang is flabbergasted by the prank.

Who is more shocked?

.......................................................................................................................................

c. Plato jogged home. Bearnice sprinted home.

Who ran the fastest?

.......................................................................................................................................

d. Bogart is outraged. Grit is irritated.

Who is angrier?

.......................................................................................................................................

e. Brick's painting was flawless. Shang High's painting was lovely.

Whose painting was better?

.......................................................................................................................................

f. Oz nibbled the pizza. Plato devoured the pizza. Bogart munched

the pizza.

Who ate the fastest?

.......................................................................................................................................

Prefixes are letters or groups of letters that are added to the beginning of words to change their meaning.

The prefix **sub-** means **under**.

sub + title = **subtitle**
meaning the secondary title,
**under the main title**

The prefix **super-** means **over**, **more**, or **beyond**.

super + glue = **superglue**
meaning a type of glue that is
**stronger than normal glue**

# 1 Transform these stories with the right prefix!

Pick the correct prefix and write the whole word in the blank to complete the sentence. Say it out loud to make sure it makes sense.

a. Grit found what he was

looking for .............................

deep underwater!

sub-　super-　merged

b. Brick promised to use his

..................................................

to fight evil.

sub-　super-　powers

c. Shang High smelled the sour milk and thought it might finally be time to go to the .................... .

sub-  super- market

d. Yin and Yang posed for the cameras like .................... .

sub-  super- stars

e. Bearnice was less than impressed that the temperature was .................... .

sub-  super- zero

Prefixes are letters or groups of letters that are added to the beginning of words to change their meaning.

The prefixes **mis**-, **un**-, and **dis**- make a word negative, often meaning **not**.

mis + hear = **mishear**     un + usual = **unusual**     dis + obey = **disobey**

meaning **to not hear** something correctly | meaning strange or **not usual** | meaning to go against or **not obey**

## 1 Transform these stories with the right prefix!

Pick the correct prefix and write the whole word in the blank to complete the sentence. Say it out loud to make sure it makes sense.

a. The kitchen was incredibly

..................................... after

Bearnice, Plato, and Armie

finished cooking dinner.

**un-**    **mis-**   tidy

b. Yang loves to

..................................... .

Her favorite way to pass the

time is surprising Yin with a

bucket of cold water!

**mis-**    **dis-**   behave

c. Shang High looked at his

lottery ticket in

........................................... .

He'd won the jackpot!

( un- )  ( dis- )  belief

d. Bogart chomped through the

rotten sandwich with delight,

but he felt very

............................................ later

that day.

( mis- )  ( un- )  well

e. Armie really .............................

performing on stage. It makes

his stomach feel as if it's full

of butterflies.

( un- )  ( dis- )  likes

Vocabulary has the power to transform any piece of writing into something exciting. Take this simple sentence:

**The boy saw the cake and ate a slice.**

By adding some adjectives and replacing a few of the words, the sentence is completely transformed. Now, it tells the reader a lot more about what happened:

The **ravenous** boy **noticed** the cake and **instantly devoured** a slice.

You need all kinds of words to tell stories. In this section, we'll learn some adjectives to help you describe cloudy weather and food flavors. We'll also learn some verbs that mean "to look," because repeating the same words all the time can make writing boring.

Knowing these words will also help you with your reading, because they are words you are likely to come across in books.

Next to each word, you will find a list of **synonyms** and **word pairs** and an empty table with two columns. Sort each word in the list into the correct column.

A **synonym** is a word that means the same or nearly the same as another word.

**Word pairs** (or collocates) are words that are often found together in speech or in writing, like **heavy rain** or **heavy suitcase**.

**heavy rain**

**heavy suitcase**

**1**

| thick | forest | book |
| fog | solid | heavy |

| synonyms | word pairs |
|----------|-----------|
| thick | fog |
| | |
| | |

## dense

*adj.* thick, solid, or heavy;
like a cloud so thick you
need a knife to cut through it

a. Extra challenge! Can you write a sentence using the word *dense*?

**2**

| sky | memories | cloudy |
| misty | sunshine | foggy |

| synonyms | word pairs |
|----------|-----------|
| | |
| | |
| | |

## hazy

*adj.* cloudy or misty;
like a fog that makes it
hard to see clearly

a. Extra challenge! Can you write a sentence using the word *hazy*?

**1**

| boring | statement | plain |
|--------|-----------|-------|
| food | tasteless | colors |

| synonyms | word pairs |
|----------|------------|
|          |            |
|          |            |
|          |            |

# bland

*adj.* plain or flavorless;
like boring food that doesn't
taste of anything

a. Extra challenge! Can you write a sentence using the word *bland*?

**2**

| fruit | sauce | sharp |
|-------|-------|-------|
| jelly | zesty | sour |

| synonyms | word pairs |
|----------|------------|
|          |            |
|          |            |
|          |            |

# tangy

*adj.* flavorful and sharp;
like the sour taste of
a grapefruit

a. Extra challenge! Can you write a sentence using the word *tangy*?

**1**

| see | suddenly | briefly |
| spot | unexpectedly | notice |

| synonyms | word pairs |
| --- | --- |
|  |  |
|  |  |
|  |  |

## glimpse

*v.* to spot or get a quick look at something; like catching sight of a mouse out of the corner of your eye

a. Extra challenge! Can you write a sentence using the word *glimpse*?

**2**

| down | peek | gaze |
| stare | curiously | inside |

| synonyms | word pairs |
| --- | --- |
|  |  |
|  |  |
|  |  |

## peer

*v.* to peek or stare; like looking over your shoulder to see what's going on

a. Extra challenge! Can you write a sentence using the word *peer*?

# SPELLING

Using the correct spelling of a word helps your reader understand exactly what you mean. In this chapter, you'll master the spellings of sounds that you might be familiar with from learning phonics. Some sounds have multiple spelling patterns, and in this book, you will practice the most important ones. You will also find some common exception words that don't follow the rules.

Vowel sounds can be long or short.
These are all sounds and spellings
you might be familiar with
from learning phonics.

## Long a sound

**ai**
rain

**ay**
hay

**a_e**
cake

## Long e sound

**ee**
feet

**ea**
dream

**e_e**
athlete

**ie**
thief

**y**
puppy

**ey**
key

## Long i sound

**igh**
n**igh**t

**i_e**
**i**c**e**

## Long o sound

**oa**
s**oa**p

**ow**
b**ow**

**ie**
p**ie**

**y**
cr**y**

**o_e**
r**o**p**e**

**oe**
t**oe**

## Long oo sound

**oo**
m**oo**n

**ou**
s**ou**p

**ue**
bl**ue**

**ew**
st**ew**

**u_e**
c**u**b**e**

**1** **Complete the words.**
Fill in the missing letters using the correct
**long a** spelling for each word.

a. Brick moved as slowly as a sn ........ l.

b. The pl ... n ... had to w ....... t three hours before it could take off.

c. Tod ......., Oz s ....... led across a sparkling l ... k ..... .

**2** **Complete the sentences.**
Circle the word with the correct
**long e** spelling for each word.

a. The   **sheap**     **sheep**   wandered

through the grassy   **valley**     **vallee**   .

b. "That   **monky**     **monkey**   stole

my   **miel**     **meal**   !" cried Oz.

c. Not even the   **chief**     **chefe**   detective

could catch the brilliant   **theef**     **thief**   .

**3** **Complete the words.**
Fill in the missing letters using the correct
**long i** spelling for each word.

a. Bearnice planned to inv ... t ... everyone to her party in Jul ..... .

b. Grit m ......... t be late ton ........... t.

c. "Wh ... would you l ....... to me?" asked Bogart.

## 4 Complete these sentences.

Circle the word with the correct **long o** spelling for each word.

a. Bearnice felt her    **phone**    **phown**    buzz

in her    **cote**    **coat**    pocket.

b. The    **yellow**    **yelloe**    team scored

the winning    **gowl**    **goal**    .

c. The    **toed**    **toad**    hopped all the way    **hoam**    **home**    .

d. The skier slid down the    **snowy**    **snoay**

**slope**    **sloap**    .

## 5 Complete these words.

Fill in the missing letters using the correct **long oo** spelling for each word.

a. Yin swept the r ........ m with a br ........ m.

b. "Do you need a tiss ........ ?" asked Armie.

c. Bearnice's missing t ........th

gr ........ back very quickly.

d. Grit got to ch ........ se

between learning the piano

and the fl .... t .... .

The **ur** sound can be written:

*n.*

**ur**

like in s**ur**f

*n.*

**ir**

like in b**ir**d

After a **w**, the **ur** sound is written:

*n.*

**or**

like in w**or**m

*n.*

**er**

like in g**er**m

## 1 Complete these words.

Fill in the missing letters using the correct **ur** spelling.

a. b ........ n

b. th ........ sty

c. p ........ ple

d. h ........ bs

e. weath ........

f. w ........ ld

## 2 Read through this passage.

Circle the words that are spelled correctly.

Oz wants to predict the **weather** **weathir** when she grows up. She thinks **weather** **weathir** predictors have the most powerful job in the **werld** **world** , because everyone believes what they say. If Oz said it was going to rain, everyone would cancel their **burthday** **birthday** parties or **berger** **burger** barbecues. If Oz said it was going to be sunny, everyone would plan trips to the **corcus** **circus** or the beach for **surfing** **sirfing** .

If Oz said it was going to rain **perple** **purple** hats on **Thursday** **Thersday** , everyone would make sure to wear matching purple shoes. Oz loved it when people listened to her, so this would be the perfect job!

The **aw sound** can be written with an **aw**—for example, dr**aw**.

When the **aw sound** is before
an **l** or **ll**, it is written with an **a**—
for example, t**a**lk or c**a**ll.

**① Complete these words.**

Fill in the missing letters using the correct **aw** spelling.
Remember, the **aw sound** can be written **aw**, or **a** (before l or ll).

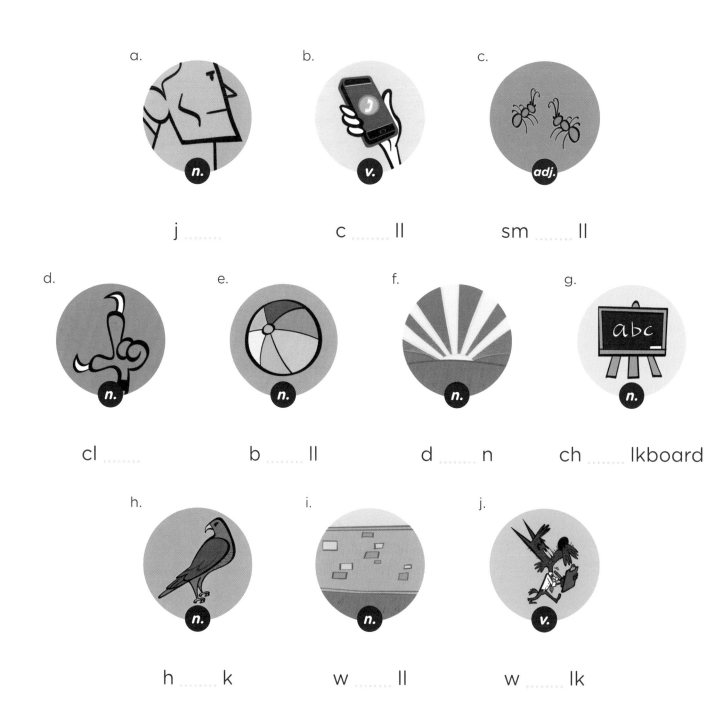

a.

*n.*

j ........

b.

*v.*

c ........ ll

c.

*adj.*

sm ........ ll

d.

*n.*

cl ........

e.

*n.*

b ........ ll

f.

*n.*

d ........ n

g.

*n.*

ch ........ lkboard

h.

*n.*

h ........ k

i.

*n.*

w ........ ll

j.

*v.*

w ........ lk

Sometimes, letters can get very shy. When they're feeling shy, they don't make a sound.

The letters **k** and **g** are very shy in front of the letter **n**. They are silent.

At the start of words, the letter **w** is very shy in front of the letter **r**. It is silent.

**EXAMPLES**

**kn**ee

**gn**aw

**wr**ap

## ① Read through this passage.

Underline all the words that have a silent **k**, **g**, or **w**.
Read them aloud to hear if the letter is silent.

It was a warm and pleasant afternoon the day the knight knocked on my door.

"Excuse me, have you seen a troublesome gnome wandering around? He has green, wrinkly skin and writes excellent songs," inquired the knight.

"No I haven't! I've been at home all day knitting a new blanket to keep my knees warm at night," I responded.

"Very good. Well, if you see him, let me know. He managed to wriggle his way through my garden fence and steal my finest petunias. My garden fence was designed to keep out creatures far larger than a gnome, you see."

"I'll be sure to let you know if I see any sign of him. Goodbye, Mr. Knight!"

As the knight walked away, a voice called to me from under my floorboards.

"That was a close call!" whispered the gnome.

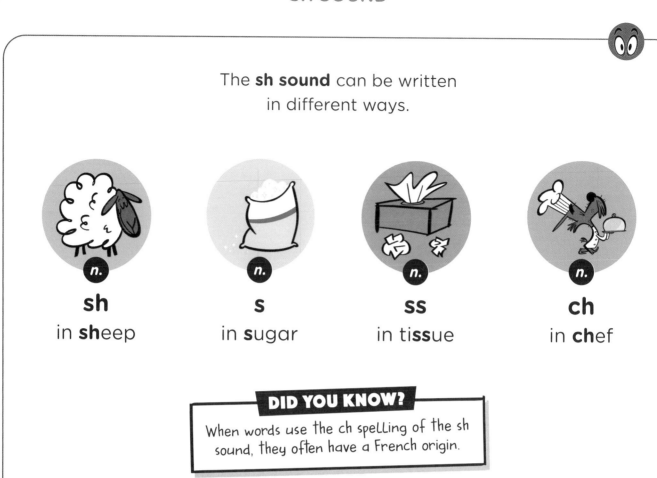

The **sh sound** can be written
in different ways.

**sh**
in **sh**eep

**s**
in **s**ugar

**ss**
in ti**ss**ue

**ch**
in **ch**ef

**DID YOU KNOW?**

When words use the ch spelling of the sh
sound, they often have a French origin.

① **Underline the sh spelling.**

Underline the letters that make the **sh** sound in each word.
The first one is done for you. Then write out each word three times.

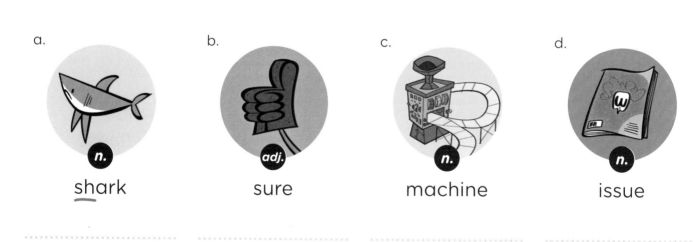

a.

shark

b.

sure

c.

machine

d.

issue

## 2 Complete the table.

Underline the letters that make the **sh** sound in each word in the box.
Then write the words under the matching spelling pattern.

| tissue | shout | sure | parachute |
| vanish | issue | machine | sugar |

| sh | s | ch | ss |
| --- | --- | --- | --- |
|  |  |  |  |
|  |  |  |  |

## 3 Complete these sentences.

Choose the correct spelling below and fill in the blanks.

mashine / machine

parachute / parashute

vanissed / vanished

chugar / sugar

**DID YOU KNOW?**
Use the options in question 2 to help you, or challenge yourself by not looking!

a. Yang escaped the scene of the crime and ........................... in

   a puff of purple smoke.

b. As Armie prepared to jump from the airplane, he really hoped

   he hadn't forgotten his ........................... .

c. "Beep boop beep boop," said the ........................... as it

   powered on.

d. Plato believed every dessert could be improved with more

   ........................... .

> **Hard g** is the first sound in words like **g**oat or **g**oal.
> **Soft g** is the first sound in words like **g**iraffe or **j**elly.
>
> **Soft g** can be found at the beginning, middle, or end of a word.
>
> At the beginning or middle of a word,
> it is usually written as **g** like **g**iraffe or **j** like **j**elly.
>
> At the end of a word, it is usually written
> as **ge** like oran**ge** or **dge** like bri**dge**.

**1** Circle the words with a soft g sound.

orange        grammar        guard

genius        angel        group

**2** Complete these words.
Fill in the blanks with **j**, **dge**, **g**, or **ge** for each word.

a. The car's en........ine made a terrible screeching noise.

b. Oz loved performing on sta.........

c. The crowd loved the musician's ori.........inal song.

d. Bogart explored the world's largest .........ungle.

e. The .........ymnast trained daily for the Olympics.

f. Yin let Yang borrow her .........acket.

g. There is a .........iant living under that bri.........

The **hard c** sound can be written **c** like **cup**, **k** like **kite**, and **ck** like **sock**.
The **soft c** sound is written **c** when followed by **e**, **i**, or **y**.
This makes an **s** sound, like in **juice**.

### REMEMBER!

Words that have a short vowel sound before the hard c end with ck, like sock.
Words that have a long vowel sound before the hard c end with k, like cheek.

**1** Circle the (soft c) and underline the hard c sound.

## circle

**2** Circle the words with a soft c sound.

calendar          caught          center

century          continue          certain

**3** Check the words that are spelled correctly.

a. kastle    ◯    castle    ◯

b. voice    ◯    voike    ◯

c. celery    ◯    selery    ◯

d. micke    ◯    mice    ◯

**REMEMBER!**

Verbs ending in -ed talk about the past. Verbs ending -ing show that something is happening (right now) or was happening (in the past).

However, not all verbs take -**ed** and -**ing** in the same way.

**1**

To most verbs, you simply add -**ed** or -**ing**.

**talk**

talk + ed → **talked**

talk + ing → **talking**

**2**

When a verb **ends in -e**, you **remove the final -e** before adding -**ed** or -**ing**.

**dance**

dance + ed → **danced**

dance + ing → **dancing**

**3**

When a verb **ends in a consonant and a -y**, you have to **change the -y to an -i** before adding -**ed**.

**carry**

carry + i + ed → **carried**

**4**

When a verb **ends in a short vowel sound followed by a consonant**, you need to **double the last letter** first before adding -**ing** or -**ed**.

g is a consonant

**hug**

short u vowel sound

hug + g + ed → **hugged**

hug + g + ing → **hugging**

**1** **Transform these verbs into the past tense with -ed.**

a. wave ➡ ......................................

b. slip ➡ ......................................

c. worry ➡ ......................................

d. ask ➡ ......................................

e. cry ➡ ......................................

f. drop ➡ ......................................

**2** **Complete these sentences.**

Fill in the missing words using the options and adding **-ing**.
Remember to adjust the spelling in the correct way.

| write | close | nod |
|-------|-------|-----|

| step | watch | slam |
|------|-------|------|

a. Yang is ...................................... her bedroom door in anger.

b. Grit is ...................................... down his secrets in invisible ink.

c. "Oh no!" cried Armie, just as he was ...................................... on the

ancient booby trap.

d. Oz was just ...................................... her eyes when she heard

a loud noise.

e. Plato is ...................................... the head chef's cooking

technique carefully.

f. Brick was ...................................... his head enthusiastically.

You can add the suffixes -**er** and -**est** to some adjectives.

The suffix -**er** changes the meaning to **more.**

Old**er** means more old.

The suffix -**est** changes the meaning to **most.**

Old**est** means the most old.

However, not all adjectives take -**er** and -**est** in the same way.

**1**

For most adjectives, you just add an -**er** or an -**est**:

small + er → **smaller**

small + est → **smallest**

**2**

For adjectives that **end in** -**e**, you remove the final -**e** before adding -**er** or -**est**:

brav~~e~~ + er  **braver**

brav~~e~~ + est → **bravest**

**3**

For adjectives that end in -**y**, you take off the -**y** and add an -**i** before adding -**er** or -**est**:

funn~~y~~ + i + er → **funnier**

funn~~y~~ + i + est  **funniest**

**4**

For adjectives that have a **short vowel sound** followed by a **consonant**, you double the last letter and then add -**er** or -**est**:

wet + t + er → **wetter**

wet + t + est → **wettest**

# 1 Add -er suffixes and fill in the blanks.

Fill in the blanks with the words below. You will need to add
or take away letters from some words before you can add the -er.

| friendly | fit | rare | safe |

a.  Grit knew he had to be ................................................ to make friends.

b.  It was much ................................................ on the boat than in the shark-

   infested ocean.

c.  The ................................................ the gem stone, the higher the price.

d.  Brick is much ................................................ than the average person.

   He runs three times a day.


# 2 Add -est suffixes and fill in the blanks.

Fill in the blanks with the words below. You will need to add
or take away letters from some words before you can add the -est.

| hot | scary | strange | lucky |

a.  "The ................................................ thing happened," said Yin, confused.

b.  This was the ................................................ haunted house in the world.

c.  When Grit won the lottery, he felt like the ................................................

   dog in the world.

d.  8,000 ice creams were sold on the ................................................ day of

   the year.

Plural nouns show that there are more than one of that noun.
There are different spelling rules to help us show this.

**1**

To turn most nouns into plural nouns, **add -s**:

cat + s → cats

**2**

When the noun ends in
-**s**, -**ch**, -**sh**, -**x**, or -**z**, **add -es**:

sandwich + es → sandwiches

**3**

When the noun ends with a **consonant**
and a -**y**, **remove -y** and **add -ies**:

party + ies → parties

**4**

For most nouns ending in -**f**, **remove -f** and **add -ves**:

leaf + ves → leaves

**1 Turn these nouns into plural nouns.**

Use the rules above to help you.

a.

*n.*
shelf

b.
*n.*
butterfly

c.

*n.*
wolf

d.

*n.*
bench

e.

n.

house

↓

........................

f.

n.

bush

↓

........................

g.

n.

elf

↓

........................

h.

n.

trophy

↓

........................

## 2 Complete these sentences.

Cross out the nouns in bold and rewrite them as plural nouns.

a. The famous group of ~~thief~~ thieves ........................ had never

been caught.

b. Plato decorated the cake with chocolate and **strawberry**

........................ .

c. Oz made three secret birthday **wish** ........................ .

d. Bogart always has an excuse to get out of washing the

**dish** ........................ .

e. Over one hundred **bunny** ........................ live in this burrow.

f. The baker makes a hundred **loaf** ........................ of bread

a day.

Some nouns form irregular plurals.
This means they do not end in -**s** or -**es**.

**1**

Some nouns change vowels:

One **foot** ➡ Two **feet**

**3**

Some nouns do not change at all:

One **sheep** ➡ Two **sheep**

**2**

Some nouns change
substantially:

One **mouse** ➡ Two **mice**

**4**

In some nouns ending in -**us**,
replace the -**us** with -**i**:

One **cactus** ➡ Two **cacti**

Irregular plurals are words we have to learn by heart,
so let's make it fun by practicing them in different ways.

**1** # Match the singular noun to its irregular plural.

Draw lines to match the nouns.

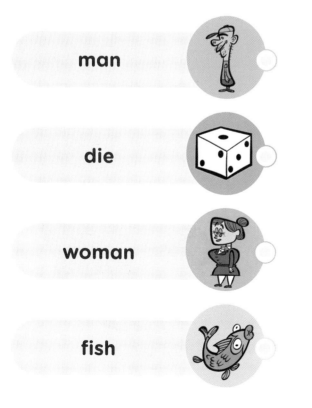

man

die

woman

fish

fish

men

dice

women

tooth

person

fungus

goose

ox

deer

child

mouse

 people

 deer

 teeth

 fungi

 children

 mice

 geese

 oxen

**EXTRA CHALLENGE!**

Can you say these words
aloud in a sentence?

Suffixes are letters or groups of letters that are
added to the end of words to change their meaning.

Sometimes, the spelling of
a root word does not change
when the suffix -**ment**, -**ness**,
-**ful**, or -**less** is added.

## quiet + ness → quietness

However, if the root word ends
with a **consonant and a -y**,
remove the -**y** and add an -**i**
before adding the suffix.

## lazy + i + ness → laziness

## ① Write the words in full.

Complete these words by adding the suffix -**ment**, -**ness**, -**ful**, or -**less**.
Don't forget to watch out for words ending in a **consonant and a -y**.

a. beauty + ful → .......................................................

b. happy + ness → .......................................................

c. hope + less → .......................................................

d. pain + ful → .......................................................

e. enjoy + ment → .......................................................

f. lonely + ness → .......................................................

g. mercy + ful → .......................................................

h. greedy + ness → .......................................................

## ② Correct the spellings!

The words ending in the suffix -**ment**, -**ness**, -**ful**, or -**less** are incorrectly spelled. Can you rewrite these words with the correct spelling?

a. Sometimes, Yang's ~~sillyness~~ _silliness_ was a bit too much for Yin to handle.

b. Yin ate a pityful dinner of one single bean.

c. Armie was not prepared for the windyness of his vacation destination.

d. Grit was left pennyless after spending the day with Yin and Yang.

e. Oz had noticed an incredible improvment in the quality of cupcakes in recent years.

Sometimes, adding the suffix **-er** does **not** mean **more**.

Adding **-er** to verbs transforms the root word into a noun.

### sing + er → singer

When the verb ends in the letter **-e**,
remove the final **-e** before adding **-er**.

**1** Transform these verbs into nouns by adding -er.

a.
**teach**
n.

b.
**garden**
n.

c.
**build**
n.

d.
**clean**
n.

e.
**play**
n.

f.
**photograph**
n.

g.
**write**
n.

h.
**farm**
n.

Adverbs **describe verbs.** Remember, a verb is a doing or being word. Adverbs describe **how** or **when** we do things.

You can turn some adjectives into **adverbs** by adding **-ly** to the end of them.

**loud + ly** ➡ **loudly**

If the adjective ends in a **-y**, like **lazy**, you first have to remove the **-y** and add an **-i** before adding **-ly**:

**laz~~y~~ + i + ly** ➡ **lazily**

If the adjective ends in **-le**, like **gentle**, you remove the **-le** and add **-ly**:

**gent~~le~~ + ly** ➡ **gently**

If the adjective ends in **-ic**, like **tragic**, you add **-ally** instead:

**tragic + ally** ➡ **tragically**

---

**1** ## Rewrite these sentences using adverbs.

The words in bold describe the action of the verb. Turn them into adverbs using the rules above. The first one is done for you.

a. "It wasn't me!" said Yang **in an innocent way**.

   *"It wasn't me!" said Yang innocently.*

b. Yin accepted the award **in a humble way**.

   .....................................................................................................

c. Armie shared his lunch **in a generous way**.

   .....................................................................................................

d. "That's really funny," said Bogart **in a sarcastic way**.

   .....................................................................................................

e. Grit barked **in a ferocious way**.

   .....................................................................................................

**REMEMBER!**

Suffixes are Letters or groups of Letters that are added to the end of words to change their meaning.

The suffix **-ation** can be added to some verbs to form a noun.

For some verbs, you just add **-ation**:

**relax + ation** → **relaxation**

For verbs that **end in -e**, you usually **remove the final -e** before adding **-ation**:

**explore + ation** → **exploration**

For verbs that **end in -ate**, you usually **remove the final -ate** before adding **-ation**:

**celebrate + ation** → **celebration**

**1** Transform these verbs into nouns by adding -ation.

a. inform → ............................................................................................

b. expect → ............................................................................................

c. public → ............................................................................................

**2** Transform these verbs into nouns by removing the final -e and adding -ation.

a. accuse → ............................................................................................

b. admire → ............................................................................................

c. invite →

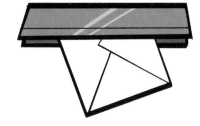

**3** Transform these verbs into nouns by removing the final -ate and adding -ation.

a. locate ➡ ...................................................................

b. donate ➡ ...................................................................

c. educate ➡ ...................................................................

**4** Complete this story.

Transform these verbs into nouns by adding -**ation**.
Don't forget to watch out for words ending in -**e** or -**ate**.

Plato couldn't sleep at all last night. He needed to memorize

a lot of **(inform)** .................................... to pass the important

**(examine)** .................................... . Plato knew there was an

**(expect)** .................................... from Mr. Teacher that he would fail,

so he was determined to prove them all wrong.

The next morning, Plato biked to the exam's **(locate)** .................................... .

He sat at his desk and nervously chewed on his pencil.

This was the most important test of his entire **(educate)**

.................................... .

Mr. Teacher stood up at the front of the hall and said, "You have

one hour to complete the science exam, starting ... now."

Plato gulped and looked around with confusion. "Science exam?"

he whispered. "But I've been studying History!"

**REMEMBER!**

Suffixes are letters or groups of letters that are added to the end of words to change their meaning. Unlike prefixes, suffixes often change the word's tense or word class.

The suffix -**ous** can be added to some nouns to turn them into adjectives.

For some nouns, you just add -**ous**:

**danger + ous** → **dangerous**

For nouns that **end in -e**, you usually **remove the final -e** before adding -**ous**:

**fame + ous** → **famous**

The suffix **-ous** means **full of**, so dangerous means **full of danger** (like a pit of snakes) and famous means having a **lot of fame** (like a celebrity chef).

**1** **Transform these nouns into adjectives by adding -ous.**

a. joy        →    .................................................

b. mountain   →    .................................................

c. villain    →    .................................................

**DID YOU KNOW!**

A villain is an evil character, like someone who wants to take over the world!

**2** **Transform these nouns into adjectives by removing the final -e and adding -ous.**

a. adventure  →    .................................................

b. nerve      →    .................................................

c. ridicule   →    .................................................

**3** **Transform these nouns into adjectives.**

a. odor        ➡ .......................................................................

b. poison      ➡ .......................................................................

c. carnivore   ➡ .......................................................................

**4** **Complete these sentences.**
Choose the correct spelling in the box and fill in the blanks.

ridiculous / ridiculeous

nervus / nervous

villainous / villanorous

adventurous / adventourous

a. Shang High's excuse for not doing his homework was absolutely

   ............................................... .

b. Bogart came up with a ............................................... plan to

   destroy the world.

c. Bearnice packed her hiking boots, climbing gear, and lasso.

   She was ready for an ............................................... vacation.

d. Armie often felt ............................................... when he spoke

   to new people.

## REMEMBER!

Suffixes are letters or groups of letters that are added
to the end of words to change their meaning.

Some suffixes sound similar but are spelled differently,
like -**sure** and -**ture**.

*n.*

trea**sure**

*n.*

na**ture**

These suffixes sound similar, but if you really
pronounce them, you can tell the difference.

The -**sure** in treasure sounds like:

# "zhur"

The -**ture** in nature sounds like:

# "chur"

## WATCH OUT!

Some words ending in the "chur" sound aren't written –ture. If the root word
already ends in –ch, then the suffix is simply –er. For example, teacher.

## 1 Complete these words.

Fill in the missing letters using the correct -**sure** or -**ture** spelling for each
word. Remember to say the word out loud to hear if it has the "zhur"
(-**sure**) or "chur" (-**ture**) sound.

a. mea .............

b. crea .............

c. plea .............

d. furni .............

e. adven .............

f. pic .............

## 2 Complete these sentences.

Fill in the blanks using the words you completed in activity 1.

a. Brick always accidentally blinks when people take

a ............................... of him.

b. Bearnice is convinced there is

a terrifying ............................... living

at the bottom of the pond.

c. Grit's pants were far too long because he

forgot to ............................... the length of his legs.

d. Yang took a lot of ............................... and delight

in causing chaos.

e. Bearnice painted all of the ............................... in the house purple.

f. Armie usually prefers to read

about an ............................... than

to go on one himself.

Some words are a little trickier to spell than others.
These words don't follow the rules we expect them to follow.

Some people call these exception words.
We call them **rebel words**.

These are words we have to learn by heart,
and it can be fun to practice them in different ways.

## 1 Copy out these rebel words.

Circle the sounds that are spelled differently from how they are pronounced. Copy out each rebel word and read it aloud.

a.

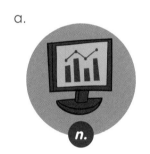

*n.*

business

b.

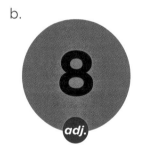

*adj.*

eight

c.

*n.*

February

d.

*n.*

island

e.

*adj.*

famous

f.

*n.*

length

g.

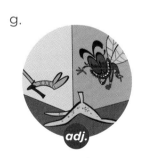

*adj.*

naughty

h.

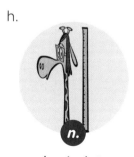

*n.*

height

## 2 Complete the sentences.

Choose the correct spelling and fill in the blanks.

a. Shang High was proud of his immense ............................................... .

**height**    **hight**

b. Oz is certain she will be ................................... when she grows up.

**famos**    **famous**

c. Armie dreams of reading on a private, secluded

............................................... .

**island**    **ailand**

d. Plato is cooking for a dinner party of ................................... people.

**ayt**    **eight**

e. Bearnice swam a full ................................... of the pool without

water wings.

**lenth**    **length**

f. Bogart started preparing his April Fools' prank in

............................................... .

**Febuary**    **February**

g. Yin is the nice twin and Yang is the ................................... twin.

**nawty**    **naughty**

h. Brick started a healthy smoothie ............................................... .

**business**    **bizness**

# READING AND WRITING

Here, you will read character-rich fiction texts and illuminating nonfiction texts. You will answer some questions about the text and some questions that ask you to practice skills that you learned in the rest of the book. At the end of this section, there are prompts to help you take your writing to the next level.

In this section, we'll be reading one of Aesop's **fables**. Take your time as you read and use the text to help you answer the questions that follow. Let's begin by learning a bit about Aesop and his fables.

## Who was Aesop?

Aesop lived in Ancient Greece around the year 600 BCE (before the common era, which means before the year 1 in most calendars). Aesop wrote fables.

Not much is known about Aesop. Some believe that he was an enslaved man who was freed after he impressed people with his stories and life lessons.

Other people believe that Aesop was not just one person, but a name given to a group of people who all told similar stories over the course of many years.

## What is a fable?

A fable is a short story that tries to teach the reader a lesson about life. Fables are similar to folktales (stories that get passed on from generation to generation), but fables always include a moral lesson.

Aesop's fables belong to the oral tradition of storytelling. This means that they were spoken instead of written down and then passed on from one person to the next. The plot and life lesson remained generally the same when they were told, but other details might be added or taken away depending on the storyteller.

Let's read the Mrs Wordsmith retelling of Aesop's fable "The Fox and the Grapes."

## The Fox and the Grapes

On a pleasant summer's evening at a quarter past seven, an elegant fox emerged from a hedge and set off at a gentle trot down a peaceful country lane.

This was not just any fox. He was one of the finest foxes for miles around, and he knew it. He had gorgeous red fur and a quick mind, which he used to get whatever he wanted. This fox could outfox anyone.

The fox was in an extremely smug mood this evening, because evening was his favorite time of the day. He knew that at seven o'clock, the farmer who lived nearby would go inside for dinner and leave his orchard completely unguarded. As the fox climbed up over the wall and into the orchard, he hoped to find endless rows of apple trees, heavy under the weight of delicious, ripe apples.

But as he searched the orchard, he found no such thing. The apples weren't ripe at all. He pulled one off a tree and grimaced at the sour taste. Yuck! Disappointed and hungry, the fox turned back the way he had come.

Just as he was about to climb back over the wall, something caught his eye. One of the trees was covered in the most beautiful vines, and on those vines hung the most tempting bunch of grapes that the fox had ever seen.

"That's more like it," smirked the fox. "I guess I do always get what I want!"

The fox fixed his gaze on the tempting grapes and jumped as high as he could, but on his first jump, he couldn't reach. He tried again, but again he didn't jump high enough. He tried a third time, but still he could not reach the lowest hanging fruit.

He couldn't believe it. A fine fox like himself should be able to get whatever he wanted. He blinked, gritted his teeth, and tried one last time, but still no luck!

"What a waste of time and effort this is!" he said loudly, looking around to check if anyone was watching. "Those grapes look disgusting! I bet they're sour! And anyway, grape skins always get stuck in my teeth."

And with that he crept away, hungrier than ever.

**DID YOU KNOW?**

The phrase "sour grapes" comes from this fable. People use this phrase when a person speaks negatively about something just because they can't have it.

**1** # True or false?

Underline the statements that are true.
Use the information in the text to help you.

a. A fable is the opposite of a folktale.

b. Aesop might have been one person or a group of people.

c. Stories in the oral tradition were spoken aloud.

**2** # Which sentence best describes the fox toward the beginning of the fable?

a. The fox is very shy.

b. The fox is very proud of himself.

c. The fox is not very clever.

**3** # Why does the fox like the evening best?

..............................................................................................................................................

..............................................................................................................................................

..............................................................................................................................................

..............................................................................................................................................

**4** # Who is the fox speaking to when he says, "That's more like it"?

a. the farmer

b. himself

c. the other animals watching

## 5 Can you order these events?

In which order did these things happen in the text? Write the numbers 1 to 4 in the boxes. If you're not sure, go back and check the text.

a.  The fox tastes an apple. ◯

b.  The fox says he doesn't like grapes. ◯

c.  The fox climbs the orchard wall. ◯

d.  The fox catches sight of the grapes. ◯

## 6 How do you think the fox feels when he can't reach the grapes?

Write one adjective to describe his feelings at that moment.

................................................................................................................................................................

## 7 Why do you think the fox says that the grapes are sour?

................................................................................................................................................................

................................................................................................................................................................

................................................................................................................................................................

................................................................................................................................................................

................................................................................................................................................................

................................................................................................................................................................

In this section, we're going to focus on reading comprehension skills when reading nonfiction texts. Reading comprehension is all about reading a text carefully, taking your time and understanding it.

First, you're going to read a **news article** about **esports**!
Take your time and read the article slowly.

Then use the text to help you answer the questions.
If you aren't sure about an answer, go back and read
the article again. All the information you need is in the text.

## VOCABULARY

### tournament

*n.* **a competition with a series of games played, where the winners of each game play against each other until one winner remains**
The final round of the tennis tournament was over in 20 minutes.

### revenue

*n.* **the amount of money earned in the sale of goods and services**
The company doubled their revenue this year by making $1 million.

### controversy

*n.* **a disagreement, debate, or cause of discussion**
There was controversy over the teacher's
decision to put the whole class in detention.

### DID YOU KNOW?

Nonfiction texts are based on
facts and are not made up
like fiction texts are.

# *Wordsmith Weekly*

## Esports' Popularity on the Rise

Esports, short for electronic sports, are multiplayer video games played competitively by professional gamers. Esports tournaments take place in huge arenas all around the world, with fans watching in person and online. Esports are becoming more and more popular, and there is a lot of money involved. In 2020, esports' worldwide revenue reached $947 million, with gamers often playing for millions in prize money.

The League of Legends World Championship final in 2019 was watched by over 4 million viewers. The tournament ran between October and November 2019 in Berlin, Madrid, and Paris. The Chinese team *FunPlus Phoenix* came in first, winning $834,375 in prize money.

There is some controversy about calling esports "sports." The Cambridge dictionary defines sport as "a game, competition, or activity needing physical effort and skill that is played or done according to rules." Esports require very minimal physical effort beyond pressing buttons, but many argue that the skill and training involved means it should be considered a sport. Some players train for over 16 hours a day.

Esports' popularity is definitely increasing. It is estimated that 439 million people watched esports events in 2020. This is over 40 million more people than in 2019, and it is believed that this will only continue to rise over the coming years.

**1 What is esports short for?**
**Check your answer.**

a. Energetic sports ◯

b. Electronic sports ◯

c. Enigmatic sports ◯

d. Electric sports ◯

> **REMEMBER!**
> If you aren't sure about an answer, go back and read the article again. ALL the information you need is in the text.

**2 In 2020, what was esports' worldwide revenue?**

........................................................................................................

........................................................................................................

**3 Where did the championship take place?**
Name three cities in which the 2019 League of Legends World Championship took place.

........................................................................................................

**4 Check the true statements.**

a. More people watched esports in 2019 than in 2020. ◯

b. An Austrian team won the 2019 League of Legends World Championship. ◯

c. The popularity of esports is increasing. ◯

**5** **What is the "controversy" that the text talks about?**

If you aren't sure about the answer, reread the text for clues.

......................................................................................................

**6** **Headings and subheadings.**

a. Why do you think the article is titled "Esports' Popularity

on the Rise"?

......................................................................................................

......................................................................................................

b. What subheading would you give the third paragraph beginning:

*There is some controversy about calling esports "sports"?*

......................................................................................................

......................................................................................................

**7** **Extra challenge! What do you think?**

"Esports aren't real sports because they don't involve any physical activity." Do you agree or disagree with this statement? Explain your answer below using full sentences.

......................................................................................................

......................................................................................................

......................................................................................................

......................................................................................................

......................................................................................................

In this section, we'll be reading a **nonfiction** text about Ancient Egypt. Take your time as you read and use the text to help you answer the questions that follow.

Some of the questions will test your understanding of the text. Some of the questions will ask you to practice skills that you learned in the rest of this book.

**DID YOU KNOW?**

Nonfiction texts are based on facts and are not made up like fiction texts are.

## VOCABULARY

### pyramid

*n.*

a huge, triangular structure that was built as a tomb for a pharaoh

### papyrus

*n.*

a material made from a water plant that was used to write or paint on

### mummification

*n.*

the process of preserving pharaohs and important animals after death

### pharaoh

*n.*

an Ancient Egyptian ruler

# LIFE IN ANCIENT EGYPT

## Where did the Ancient Egyptians live?

The Ancient Egyptian civilization began 5,000 years ago and lasted for around 3,000 years. The Ancient Egyptians lived along the banks of the Nile. The Nile is the longest river on Earth. It runs through the continent of Africa, through Uganda, Tanzania, and Kenya, before ending in the Mediterranean Sea.

Living on a river had many benefits for the Ancient Egyptians. It was a source of food and water and a way to transport things over long distances by boat.

## What jobs did the Ancient Egyptians do?

Life was tough for those who were not wealthy, with children as young as 12 going to work. People could be farmers, bakers, scribes, priests, doctors, craftsmen, or merchants, to name a few. Most people did the same job that their parents did.

There was no such thing as school, unless you were training to become a priest or a scribe. Most people could not read or write, but those who could used a writing system called hieroglyphs. Hieroglyphs are a system of pictures and symbols that represent sounds or groups of sounds.

## What did the Ancient Egyptians eat?

The banks of the Nile were (and still are) a very good place to grow crops for food. The banks of the river flooded every year, and when this happened, the water left behind nutrient-rich silts that made the soil very fertile.

What you ate as an Ancient Egyptian depended on how wealthy you were. Richer, more powerful people like pharaohs and priests would have eaten a luxurious diet of meat, fruit, vegetables, and cakes. Farmers and other poorer people lived on more basic foods like beans, bread, fish, onions, and garlic.

A more interesting question might be, what did Ancient Egyptians not eat? Many of the most common foods that we eat today would have been completely unfamiliar to people in Ancient Egypt, even things like bananas, potatoes, rice, and tomatoes! These ingredients had not been discovered yet by people living in Egypt.

## What did the Ancient Egyptians believe in?

Religion was an important part of Ancient Egyptian civilization. The people were ruled by pharaohs and worshiped over 2,000 gods and goddesses.

The afterlife was very important to Ancient Egyptians. They would preserve the bodies of important people through mummification and bury them in huge tombs filled with their favorite belongings. For very important people, such as pharaohs, these tombs were built in the shape of pyramids.

## 1 True or false?

Underline the statements that are true. Use the information in the text to help you.

a. The Ancient Egyptians lived mainly on mountains.

b. The Ancient Egyptians used boats.

c. The Nile River flows through more than one modern-day country.

d. The Ancient Egyptians traveled long distances by highway.

e. The Ancient Egyptians worshiped over 2,000 gods and goddesses.

f. Pharaohs were buried in tombs shaped like cubes.

## 2 What does this mean?

"Life was tough for people who were not wealthy."

Circle the correct answer.

a. Wealthy people worked hard.

c. Poorer people had an easy life.

b. Poorer people lived a harder life than richer people.

d. There were no poor people.

## 3 What kinds of jobs did the Ancient Egyptians do?

Circle all the correct answers.

farmer     electrician     baker     priest

bus driver     doctor     merchant     TV presenter

**4** **Why were the banks of the Nile a good place to grow food?**

Circle the correct answer.

because the
soil was fertile

because
food grows
underwater

because the soil
was very dry

**5** **Fact or opinion?**

Underline the statements that are facts.

a. The Nile runs through Africa.

b. The Ancient Egyptians ate the best food.

c. People started work in Ancient Egypt at the age of 12.

> **REMEMBER!**
>
> A fact is a statement that is true. It is true no matter who says it.
>
> An opinion is an expression of how a person feels or what they think about something. Opinions change depending on who is speaking.

**6** **What is the purpose of this text?**

a. to inform you about Ancient Egypt

b. to teach you how to build a pyramid

c. to persuade you to travel to Egypt

**7** **What items do you think a pharaoh might be buried with?**

Give examples of six precious things below.

.........................................................................................................

.........................................................................................................

........................................................................................

........................................................................................

........................................................................................

........................................................................................

........................................................................................

........................................................................................

**8** **Complete these sentences.**

Match the two halves of these compound sentences together.
Use the coordinating conjunctions **and**, **or**, and **but** to help you.

a. The Nile was a source of food

**but** those who could used hieroglyphs.

b. The Ancient Egyptians did not eat rice

**and** they worshiped over 2,000 gods and goddesses.

c. Most people could not read or write

**and** it was also used to transport things by boat.

d. A 12-year-old in Ancient Egypt might go to work as a farmer

**or** they might go to work as a baker.

e. The people were guided by religion

**but** they did eat fish.

In this section, we're going to focus on reading comprehension skills when reading **fiction** texts.

Reading comprehension is all about reading a text carefully, taking your time and understanding it.

Reading longer texts helps you build up your reading stamina and fluency.

**DID YOU KNOW?**

Fiction texts are made up and come from the writer's imagination.

First, we're going to learn about how stories are structured.

Then we will learn some new words that will help us when we get to the reading.

Once you have read through these new words, turn the page and read the story about Yin and Yang's silly argument and how Grit puts an end to it.

Finally, use the text to help you answer the questions. If you aren't sure about an answer, go back and read the text again.

Stories are often made up of an opening, a build-up, a climax, and a resolution.

This is sometimes called a **story mountain** because of how the plot builds up and then comes down when a resolution is found.

**DID YOU KNOW?**

The hook is a technique used in the openings of stories to "hook" the reader's attention in order to keep them reading on.

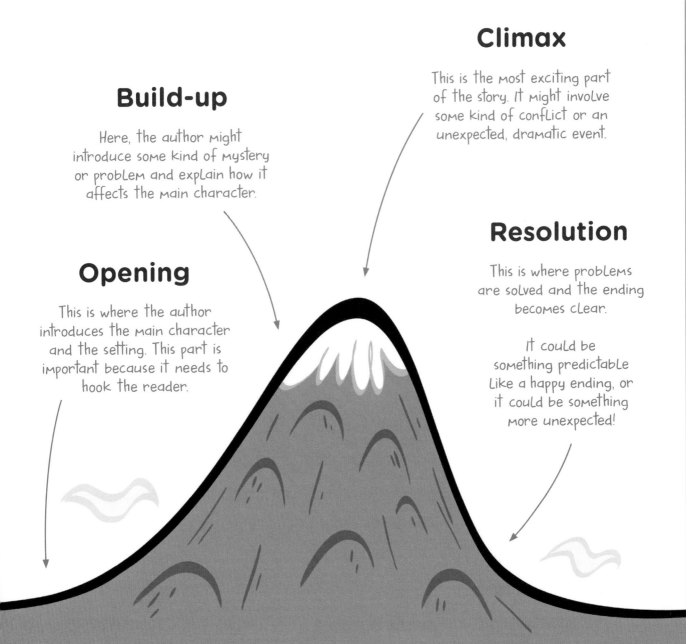

## Climax

This is the most exciting part of the story. It might involve some kind of conflict or an unexpected, dramatic event.

## Build-up

Here, the author might introduce some kind of mystery or problem and explain how it affects the main character.

## Resolution

This is where problems are solved and the ending becomes clear.

It could be something predictable like a happy ending, or it could be something more unexpected!

## Opening

This is where the author introduces the main character and the setting. This part is important because it needs to hook the reader.

Now, let's look at some words
that will help us with the reading!

# bicker

*v.* to argue over silly things;
like sisters arguing about nothing

### WORD PAIRS

bicker **constantly**
bicker **playfully**
bicker **childishly**

# squeal

*v.* to wail or yelp; like when someone makes a
high-pitched sound when they are surprised

### WORD PAIRS

squeal **loudly**
squeal **excitedly**
squeal **shrilly**

# abrasive

*adj.* harsh and grating; like a horrible noise
that makes your hair stand on end

### WORD PAIRS

abrasive **voice**
abrasive **personality**
abrasive **siren**

# feud

*n.* a long disagreement or argument;
like people fighting about the same
thing over and over again

### WORD PAIRS

**angry** feud
**bitter** feud
**never-ending** feud

# assertive

*adj.* forceful or self-confident; like someone
who makes sure they always get their way

### WORD PAIRS

assertive **voice**
assertive **salesperson**
assertive **stance**

# pungent

*adj.* very strong and smelly; like the stench
of sweaty shoes after a long workout

### WORD PAIRS

pungent **smell**
pungent **sauce**
pungent **feet**

## Bickering Sisters

Grit was looking forward to a lazy day at home. He sat in his favorite spot on the couch and put his feet up. Everything was peaceful. Just as he was about to close his eyes, Yin and Yang burst into the room. The two tiger sisters were in the middle of one of their worst **feuds** yet. They'd been arguing for hours.

Grit was wearing his headphones, but even with his gardening podcast turned up to full volume, he still couldn't block out the sound of their bickering.

Grit didn't like it when they were like this. It was always the same story! Yin claimed that Yang had started it. Yang claimed that Yin had started it. They would call each other names until eventually it all ended in tears. Grit rolled his eyes and pulled off his headphones.

"... And you smell like Brick's gym socks!" Yang was **squealing**, in a voice that was as high-pitched as car tires dragging on pavement.

"Well, you're ... you're ... you smell like a **pungent** old cheese and anchovy sandwich!!!" yelped Yin, in a voice that was as **abrasive** as nails on a chalkboard.

"Enough!" said Grit, in his deepest, most **assertive** voice. "I've had it up to here with you two. What are you fighting about this time?"

Yin and Yang froze and then looked at him. Grit crossed his arms in frustration.

"Something about ..." began Yang, pointing at her sister. "She said ... Um ... I ... I can't remember ..."

"What happened was ..." Yin interrupted and then fell silent. "Well ... neither can I ..."

Yin and Yang looked at each other and then back at Grit, who was clearly not impressed. Suddenly, to Grit's surprise, the two tigers burst into fits of giggles.

"I've had it up to here with you two!" said Yang, crossing her arms and doing her best Grit impression.

"Enough!" growled Yin, trying and failing to hold back her laughter. The twins laughed so hard that they collapsed into a giggling heap.

Grit shrugged and put his headphones back on. He wasn't sure how, but he seemed to have made things better.

**1** **What was Grit trying to listen to with his headphones?**

...................................................................................

...................................................................................

**2** **True or false?**

a.  This was the first time Yin and Yang had ever argued. ...............

b.  Grit started the argument. ...........................

c.  Yin and Yang are sisters. .............................

**3** **Opening, build-up, climax, or resolution?**
Can you draw a line from each of these events in the story to the correct story stage?

| opening | build up | climax | resolution |

a.
Yin and Yang start laughing and forget their argument.

b.
Grit pulls off his headphones and says "Enough!"

c.
Grit is relaxing on the couch.

d.
Yin and Yang burst into the room.

**4** **How do you think Grit feels at the end of the story?**
Write down one word to describe Grit's feelings.

...................................................................................

**5** **How do you think Yin**
   **and Yang feel about each other?**

Friends and family sometimes bicker, but arguments don't last forever.
Circle how you think the twins usually feel about each other.

> They don't know
> each other.

> They love
> each other.

> They do not like
> each other at all.

Remember, a simile compares two things using the words **as** or **like**.

**EXAMPLES**

The giraffe was **as** tall
**as** a skyscraper.

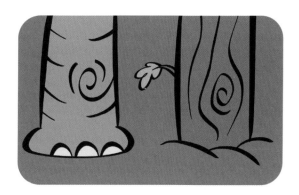

The elephant's legs
were **like** tree trunks.

**6** **Copy the simile from the text.**

a. Yang says Yin smells like ........................................ .

b. Yin says Yang smells like ........................................ .

c. Yin's voice was as ........................................ as

........................................ .

**7** **What do these similes mean?**

Match the simile from the text to a sentence that has a similar meaning.
Use the vocabulary in each simile to help you work out the meaning.

Yin spoke very slowly.

Yin's voice was as abrasive as nails on a chalkboard.

Yin wouldn't stop talking about nails and chalkboards.

Yin's voice was grating and unpleasant.

Yin says that Yang smells strongly.

Yin says that Yang smells like a pungent old cheese and anchovy sandwich.

Yin says that Yang has eaten a sandwich.

Yin says Yang likes cheese and anchovy sandwiches.

## 8 Finish the similes!

These similes are only half written.
Complete them with whatever you like!

a. Bearnice's snoring sounded like

......................................................................................................................

......................................................................................................................

......................................................................................................................

b. Oz stood as still as a

......................................................................................................................

......................................................................................................................

......................................................................................................................

c. Plato's cooking smelled like

......................................................................................................................

......................................................................................................................

......................................................................................................................

d. Shang High's bedroom was as messy as

.................................................................................................

.................................................................................................

.................................................................................................

.................................................................................................

.................................................................................

In this section, we'll be reading an **instructional text** that teaches the reader how to do something. Take your time as you read and use the text to help you answer the questions that follow. Some of the questions will ask you to practice skills that you learned in the rest of this book.

**REMEMBER!**

Nonfiction texts are based on facts and teach something to the reader.

**VOCABULARY**

**experiment**
a scientific test to discover something new or demonstrate a known fact

**volcano**
a mountain from which lava, gases, and dust are forced out of in an eruption

**lava**
hot liquid rock

**eruption**
when a volcano forces out lava, gases, and dust

## How to make a model erupting volcano at home

The largest volcano on Earth is 22,615 feet (6,893 meters) tall. The model you will build using these instructions isn't quite as large (approximately 22,614.1 feet [6,892.8 meters] smaller), but it will be much safer!

## What you will need: building the model volcano

- 16 oz (500 ml) empty plastic bottle
- 11×17-inch cardstock paper
- Scissors
- Tape or glue
- Pens, pencils, paint, paintbrushes, and any other crafting materials you like!

## What you will need: the eruption

- 1 tablespoon baking soda
- 1 tablespoon dishwashing liquid
- 3 tablespoons water
- 1 teaspoon red food coloring
- 4 oz (120 ml) vinegar
- 2 bowls

**WARNING!**

This can get messy, so we recommend you carry out this experiment outside!

## Method

1. In the middle of the cardstock paper, draw around the bottleneck and cut out the circle.

2. Wrap the paper around the bottle to form a cone shape, leaving the lid area open through the cut-out circle.

3. Tape or glue the paper into the cone shape.

4. Cut away the base so the cone sits flat.

5. Use your pens, pencils, paint, paintbrushes, and other crafting materials to decorate the cone to look like a volcano.

6. Wait for your decorations to fully dry.

7. In the first bowl, mix the baking soda, dishwashing liquid, and water.

8. Pour this mixture into the bottle in your volcano.

9. In your second bowl, mix the vinegar and red food coloring.

10. Pour the vinegar mixture into the volcano and watch as it erupts!

# 1 Number these instructions.
Order these instructions from 1 to 5.

a. Watch as the volcano erupts! ◯

b. Mix the baking soda, dishwashing liquid, and water. ◯

c. Pour the baking soda mixture into the volcano. ◯

d. Mix the vinegar and red food coloring. ◯

e. Pour the vinegar mixture into the volcano. ◯

# 2 Why should you do this experiment outside?

....................................................................................................

....................................................................................................

# 3 What don't you need for this experiment?
Cross out all the items you **do not** need to make an erupting volcano at home.

| | | |
|---|---|---|
| **11×17 cardstock** | **Scissors** | **Hair dryer** |
| **Vinegar** | **Recipe book** | **Black pepper** |

# 4 How tall is the largest volcano on Earth?

....................................................................................................

**5** **Circle the imperatives in these instructions.**

Instructions contain imperative (or bossy) verbs, like **pour**, **catch**, and **run**. Which of the words below are imperatives?

a.  Cut away the base so the cone sits flat.

b.  Wait for your decorations to fully dry.

c.  In the first bowl, mix the baking soda, dishwashing liquid, and water.

**6** **What does erupt mean?**

**7** **Why make a miniature model of a volcano?**

Explain why the volcano you build at home has to be so much smaller than a real volcano.

**8** **What is the author's purpose?**

The author's purpose is their reason for writing the text. Circle what you think this author's purpose is.

**to entertain**         **to instruct**         **to persuade**

**9** **Now it's your turn!**

Think of something that you are an expert at doing. It could be something you do every day, like brushing your teeth or getting dressed. Now, write some detailed instructions that explain how to do it. Remember to make your instructions precise and to put them in a logical order.

In this section, we'll be looking at a **poem**. Take your time as you read and use the poem to help you answer the questions that follow.

Remember, poems express a feeling, an idea, or a story.
An important thing to remember about poems is that they aren't always written in full sentences, but they are usually written in **lines**.

The lines in a poem can be grouped together to make **verses**.
In poems, verses work a bit like paragraphs. Some poems rhyme.
In poems that **rhyme**, the lines end with words that end
in the same sound, like **walk** and **talk**.

# scowl

*v.* to frown in an angry way;
like the expression you pull when
you get into an argument

**WORD PAIRS**

scowl **angrily**
scowl **threateningly**

# constant

*adj.* continuous or happening
all the time; like a phone
call that never ends

**WORD PAIRS**

constant **laughter**
constant **chatter**

# astonished

*v.* surprised or amazed;
like when you've seen something
you can't believe

--- WORD PAIRS ---

astonished **eyes**
astonished **silence**

# ravenous

*adj.* hungry or starving;
when you feel like you could eat
an entire dinner in one bite

--- WORD PAIRS ---

ravenous **dog**
ravenous **appetite**

# audacious

*adj.* bold and daring; like
someone brave enough to dive
into a pool full of sharks

--- WORD PAIRS ---

audacious **stunt**
audacious **move**

## Upside Down and Back to Front

Grumpy old Grit sighed and scowled,
He was known as a constant complainer.
His day had gone from bad to worse,
And was about to get much stranger.

"Argh!" screamed Grit, as he lost his footing,
And into a mirror he flew.
He expected to bump his head on the glass,
But instead, he fell right through.

Grit looked up and blinked, astonished,
The world seemed to have changed.
On the surface, this place looked like home,
But it was all just a little more strange.

He ate some candy, but they tasted salty,
And when he walked left, he went right.
When he jumped up, instead he sank down,
And the sun was as dark as the night.

He watched as a fish swam past on land,
And admired purple trees and pink rocks.
Even his friends seemed a little bit odd,
As he sniffed Brick's sweet-smelling socks.

Armie was audacious and Oz was shy,
And Plato's ravenous hunger decreased.
Bearnice was graceful and Brick was weak,
And Bogart dreamed of world peace.

As Grit paused to take it all in,
He stood with a smile, not a frown.
For the best thing about this backward world,
Was that it turned his mood upside down!

**1 What does this poem's title mean?**

Write down why you think this poem is named "Upside Down and Back to Front."

....................................................................

....................................................................

**2 Can you think of any other titles for this poem?**

Write down two alternate titles for this poem.

....................................................................

....................................................................

....................................................................

....................................................................

**3 Which words tell you that Grit is in a bad mood?**

Write down the three words in the first line of the poem that tell you about Grit's mood.

....................................................................

....................................................................

....................................................................

**4 What does the phrase "lost his footing" mean?**

If you're unsure, use context clues from the sentences around this phrase in the poem.

....................................................................

....................................................................

**5** **How does Grit feel when he "loses his footing"?**
Use the information in the poem to work out what Grit was feeling at this moment.

........................................................................................

........................................................................................

........................................................................................

**6** **Which word in the second verse is a synonym of hit?**
Remember, a synonym is a word that means the same or nearly the same as another word.

........................................................................................

**7** **What does Grit taste when he eats candy in the upside down world?**

........................................................................................

**8** **What is unusual about this line?**
"He watched as a fish swam past on land"

........................................................................................

........................................................................................

........................................................................................

**9** **What are the clues that Grit had entered into a strange world?**

Check all the strange things that happened in the poem.

a. There was a fish swimming on land.

b. Grit tripped over.

c. Grit walked left.

d. Grit tried to jump up, but instead sank down.

e. The trees were purple.

**10** **Match the characters with the adjectives.**

Draw lines from the character names to the adjectives used to describe them in the poem.

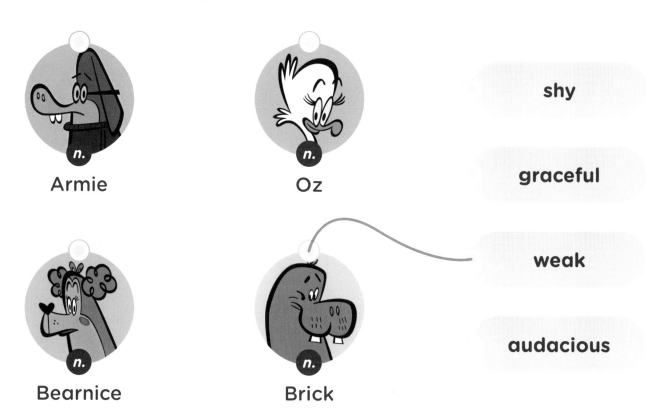

| | | shy |
| Armie *n.* | Oz *n.* | graceful |
| | | weak |
| Bearnice *n.* | Brick *n.* | audacious |

## 11  How do you know these descriptions are unusual?

Write down the phrase from the fifth verse that tells you that Armie, Oz, Bearnice, and Brick are not usually described in this way.

......................................................................................................................................................................

......................................................................................................................................................................

## 12  Now it's your turn!

Write three sentences about what you might see, hear, smell, or taste if you were in a strange opposite world. For an extra challenge, see if you can make your lines rhyme!

......................................................................................................................................................................

......................................................................................................................................................................

......................................................................................................................................................................

......................................................................................................................................................................

......................................................................................................................................................................

......................................................................................................................................................................

......................................................................................................................................................................

......................................................................................................................................................................

......................................................................................................................................................................

......................................................................................................................................................................

......................................................................................................................................................................

Now it's time to apply everything you've learned so far and get writing! In this section, you will write **a short story** based on a writing prompt.

When it's finished, this story will have four paragraphs: **an opening**, **a build-up**, **a climax**, and **a resolution**. Refer to the story mountain on page 141 for more information on each section.

Your first prompt is to

# write about Oz traveling through the jungle and finding a dangerous snake.

The first two paragraphs (the **opening** and the **build-up**) are written for you. It is your job to write the next two paragraphs (the **climax** and the **resolution**).

## Opening

This is where the author introduces the main character and the setting. This part is important because it needs to hook the reader. Here, we introduced Oz and the jungle.

*Oz's legs ached as she trudged through the scorching hot jungle. She had been traveling alone for three weeks in search of a mysterious flower that could cure any sickness. She was determined to succeed.*

## Build-up

Here, the author might introduce some kind of mystery or problem and explain how it affects the main character. We have described the mysterious noises of the jungle and how Oz feels about them.

*Oz resisted the urge to scratch her dozens of mosquito bites as she stepped deeper into the dense jungle.*

*Every now and then, she heard mysterious noises from behind the trees and leaves rustling. She hoped she would reach the other side soon.*

# 1 Climax

Now it's your turn! This is the most exciting part of the story. Here, you will describe the moment when Oz discovers the snake. To help you write this paragraph, here are some writing goals:

a. Use an adverbial phrase to show how quickly or slowly something happened—for example, **suddenly**, **in a flash**, or **in the blink of an eye**.

b. Use an exclamation mark to show an exciting moment—for example, "Then they heard a piercing scream!"

## ② Resolution

This is where problems are solved and the ending becomes clear. Here, you will need to describe what Oz does after she sees the snake and how she feels about it. To help you write this paragraph, here are some writing goals:

a. Use a sentence that consists of two clauses joined by a conjunction—for example, **and**, **or**, or **but**.

b. Use at least two adjectives (words that describe nouns) to add descriptive detail—for example, **nervous**, **afraid**, **poisonous**, or **clever**.

Your next writing prompt is to

# write about Bogart's next big scheme to take over the world.

The first two paragraphs (the **opening** and the **build-up**) are written for you. It is your job to write the next two paragraphs (the **climax** and the **resolution**).

## Opening

This is where the author introduces the main character and the setting. This part is important because it needs to hook the reader. Here, we introduced Bogart and his previous schemes to take over the world.

*Bogart had tried and failed to take over the world 146 times, but he was certain that this time was going to be different. He'd tried all the standard world domination techniques in the past, including mind-control, robots, and a highly trained army of caterpillars. None of them had worked.*

## Build-up

Here, the author might introduce some kind of mystery or problem and explain how it affects the main character. We have described Bogart's mysterious and cunning plan!

*This time, Bogart was going to try something completely new that no one would ever see coming. He spent weeks in a laboratory working on a cunning plan until he finally perfected it. He was going to create a thousand copies of himself to form an army of Bogarts!*

## ③ Climax

Now it's your turn! This is the most exciting part of the story.
Here, you will describe what happens when Bogart tries to use his
Bogart army to take over the world. To help you write this paragraph,
here are some writing goals:

a. Use at least two adverbs (words that describe verbs)
to add descriptive details—for example, **softly**, **carefully**,
**angrily**, or **anxiously**.

b. Use direct speech using inverted commas—for example,
**"Who are you?" asked Bogart.**

# 4 Resolution

This is where problems are solved and the ending becomes clear. Here, you will describe what happens to Bogart at the end of the story. Does he succeed or fail in taking over the world? To help you write this paragraph, here are some writing goals:

a. Use two words to describe the sensory details of how something feels, tastes, sounds, looks, or smells—for example, **loud**, **sour**, **stinking**, or **colorful**.

b. Use a word with the mis-, un-, or dis- prefix—for example, **mishear**, **unusual**, or **disobey**.

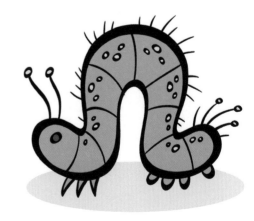

Now that you've written your own stories, you're
more than ready to edit someone else's!

① **Read through the short story below.**

All the errors in this text have been underlined, and it's your job to fix
them using skills that you learned in the rest of this book. The underlined
mistakes include spelling, punctuation, and grammar errors.

Shang Highs day was perfectly ordinary until it started

raining carrots. "What on earth is going on? cried Shang

High as he ran to take shelter under a tree. The whether

forecast certainly had'nt predicted this. Five minutes later,

the carrots finally stopped falling. "Phew," thought Shang

High as he stepped back out into the open. Then the first

banana fell. Then an orange a pepper an apple an apricot

and a lot of cabbages followed. Fruits and vegetables were

falling from the sky at a alarming rate.

Shang High retreated to his shelter

and smiled. He picked up an fallen

apple, took a bite, and waited for

the storm to pass.

## 2 Extra challenge!

We've already edited to make corrections. Now let's try editing to improve a text. Add two more sentences to describe the fruit that was falling from the sky.

Don't forget to use adjectives (like **enormous** or **tangy**) and adverbs (like **suddenly** or **loudly**) to make your sentences more exciting.

# HANDWRITING

In this section, you will get the chance to practice the most common handwriting joins. Being able to join your letters makes your writing faster and easier to read.

# JOINING LETTERS

In this section, we are going to practice how to join letters. This skill can make your writing faster and clearer. Joins connect the ending of the first letter to the beginning of the second letter. We are going to practice four different joins.

Before you start, remember to:

Sit comfortably with your
back straight and your
feet on the floor.

Sharpen your pencil
and hold it properly, with your fingers
close to the sharpened point.

If you're writing with your right hand,
tilt the page slightly to the left, and if you're
writing with your left hand, tilt the page slightly
to the right.

ascender ⟶ dog   ↕ X-height

baseline   ⟵ descender

# 1 Let's get practicing!

Before learning how to best join different letters, let's warm up by first writing out all the letters of the alphabet.

a a · b b c c · d d ·

e e · f f g g · h h

i i · j j · k k l l

m m · n n o o ·

p p · q q · r r · s s ·

t t · u u · v v ·

w w · x x ·

y y · z z ·

The first join is a diagonal
going from the baseline height
of the first letter to the x-height
of the second letter.

**1 Practice the first join.**

Follow the arrows to trace the letters in the example above.
Then practice writing the letters below, starting from the dot.

a.
an *an*

b.
am *am*

c.
as *as*

d.
ed *ed*

e.
es *es*

f.
in *in*

g.
iy *iy*

The second join is a diagonal going from the baseline of the first letter to the x-height of the second letter and continues to the top of the ascender of the second letter.

**2** **Practice the second join.**

Follow the arrows to trace the letters in the example above.
Then practice writing the letters below, starting from the dot.

a. *it* *it*

b. *if* *if*

c. *el* *el*

d. *et* *et*

e. *uf* *uf*

f. *ul* *ul*

g. *ch* *ch*

The third join is a horizontal line going from the x-height of the first letter to the x-height of the second letter.

**3** **Practice the third join.**

Follow the arrows to trace the letters in the example above.
Then practice writing the letters below, starting from the dot.

a.    on   on

b.    wi   wi

c.    rm   rm

d.    ow   ow

e.    rv   rv

f.    fu   fu

g.    fy   fy

The fourth join is a diagonal going from the x-height of the first letter to the top of the ascender of the second letter.

**4** **Practice the fourth join.**

Follow the arrows to trace the letters in the example above.
Then practice writing the letters below, starting from the dot.

a.  ok  ok

b.  ot  ot

c.  ol  ol

d.  wl  wl

e.  wh  wh

f.  rb  rb

g.  rh  rh

**5** Now practice writing these words
that contain all the joins.

a. draw draw

b. our our

c. hour hour

d. know know

e. find find

f. catch catch

g. leave leave

h. fruit fruit

i. earth earth

j. often *often*

k. answer *answer*

l. heard *heard*

m. arrive *arrive*

n. early *early*

o. famous *famous*

p. appear *appear*

q. actual *actual*

r. heart *heart*

s. island *island*

**Page 10**

**1 Common nouns:** book, dentist, dog, tree, leg, city, blanket
**Proper nouns:** Grit, Nigeria, Cairo, Wednesday, December

**2 a. Common noun:** kitchen
**Proper nouns:** Yin, Yang
**b. Common noun:** tacos
**Proper nouns:** Plato, Tuesday
**c. Common noun:** friends
**Proper nouns:** Germany, April

**Page 11**

**1** the deep blue ocean, the juggling ball, a sour and juicy lemon, a chocolate chip cookie

**2 Your answers might include:**
**a.** the soft bed with plump pillows
**b.** the famous school
**c.** a sweltering hot summer
**d.** the thousand-year-old volcano
**e.** the snowy mountain
**f.** a growling tiger

**Pages 12-13**

**1 a.** Brick loves onions and he has horrible breath.
**b.** The pizza is covered in green slime. It is disgusting.
**c.** Yin and Yang are rowing across rough water. They are terrified.
**d.** Bearnice feels as though she has a thousand things to do.

**Pages 14-15**

**1** He runs      The friends run
I run      You run
Bearnice runs      They run
We run      Yin and Yang run

**2 a.** tiptoes   **b.** slide   **c.** loves
**d.** forgets   **e.** opens   **f.** change

**3 Your answers might include:**
**a.** Brick **collects** seashells.

**b.** Yang **orders** Ying to make them both lunch.
**c.** The friends **lose** the diamond but **agree** to lie about it.

**Pages 16-17**

**1 a.** adored      **b.** touched
**c.** remembered      **d.** believed

**2 a.** wants      **b.** recognize
**c.** imagines      **d.** hate

**3 a.** Armie climbed to the top of the tallest mountain.
**b.** Grit aimed his slingshot at a buzzing beehive.
**c.** Bearnice relaxed in an indulgent mud bath.
**d.** Shang High delivered pizza all around the world.

**Pages 18-19**

**1 a.** sing sang, sit sat, sleep slept, fall fell, drink drank, forget forgot

**2 a.** Armie sat alone in the perfect spot to quietly read his favorite book.
**b.** Plato drank the juice from an extremely sour lemon.
**c.** Brick forgot to check the measurements of his vacation home.
**d.** Plato slept absolutely terribly.

**Pages 20-21**

**1 a.** lost   **b.** borrowed   **c.** chases
**d.** ate   **e.** follows   **f.** walked

**2** ride > rode
makes > made
have > had

**Pages 22-23**

**1 a.** an   **b.** a   **c.** an
**d.** a   **e.** an   **f.** an

**2 a.** a **or** the   **b.** the
**c.** a **or** the   **d.** the
**e.** a **or** the   **f.** an, a, a **or** the, the, the

**Pages 24-25**

1  **Main clauses:** Grit shouted loudly, Bearnice woke up early, she loves to dance
**Subordinate clauses:** when he was late, after driving for four hours, until it struck midnight

2  **a.** because he missed his bus.
**b.** until he fell asleep.
**c.** after being chased by a tiger.
**d.** after traveling for five minutes.
**e.** as she stepped onto the moon.
**f.** because it was too prickly.

**Pages 26-27**

1  **a.** and  **b.** but  **c.** or
**d.** and  **e.** but  **f.** but

2  **a.** Yin was irritated with Yang
**and** Yang was furious with Yin.
(**but** is also correct)
**b.** Bearnice knew Armie was thirsty,
**but** she refused to share her water.
(**and** is also correct)
**c.** Armie may be an inventor when he
grows up **or** he may be an engineer.
**d.** Oz is a beautiful singer **and** Grit is a
talented pianist. (**but** is also correct)
**e.** Shang High's room was a mess,
**but** he refused to clean it.
(**and** is also correct)

**Pages 28-29**

1  **a.** so
**b.** until
**c.** when
**d.** because
**e.** After

2  **Your answers might include:**
**a.** My best friend loves to play chess
because he always wins.
**b.** My best friend bikes to school when
it is sunny.
**c.** My best friend scored the winning

goal because she is very fast.

**Pages 30-31**

1  moldy, rapid, brilliant, overpriced

2  ancient castle, healthy breakfast,
shimmering lake, furry monster, strict
teacher, minuscule mouse

3  **Your answers might include:**
**a.** nauseating    **b.** vibrant
**c.** delectable    **d.** chirping

**Pages 32-33**

1  **a.** angrily, wildly, usually, daily

2  **a.** bravely   **b.** nervously   **c.** kindly

3  **a.** nervously   **b.** cautiously
**c.** Sometimes **d.** angrily

**Pages 34-35**

1  **a.** very quietly, yesterday afternoon,
really happy

2  **Your answer might include:**
**a.** Armie read three books a day.
**b.** The waiter walked away from our
table.
**c.** The ocean is vast and blue.
**d.** Yin and Yang slept all day.

3  **Your answer might include:**
**a.** In the morning
**b.** Completely exhausted
**c.** Trembling with excitement
**d.** As soon as she could
**e.** At the bottom of the sea
**f.** Under the floorboards

**Pages 36-37**

1  **Command:** Wash your hands.
**Statement:** Grit is very hungry.
**Question:** What time is dinner?
**Exclamation:** What a delicious meal
this is!

2  **a.** That is Bearnice.   **b.** They are tired.
**c.** She is excited.        **d.** I am ready.

**3 Your answer might include:**
**Statement:** I had a sandwich for lunch.
**Question:** What was in the sandwich?
**Command:** Eat the sandwich.
**Exclamation:** What a spicy sandwich this is!

## Pages 40-41

**1 a.** wasn't    **b.** we're    **c.** didn't
**d.** shouldn't    **e.** you'll    **f.** I'm
**g.** she's    **h.** won't

**2 a.** shouldn't    **b.** I'm    **c.** won't
**d.** wasn't    **e.** didn't    **f.** You'll
**g.** We're    **h.** She's

## Pages 42-43

**1 a.** Plato's spoon    **b.** James' garden
   **c.** Armie's pencil    **d.** Bearnice's pillow
   **e.** Chris' phone    **f.** Bogart's plan

**2 a.** The teachers' water
   **b.** The school's desk
   **c.** The women's plants
   **d.** Tobias' coat
   **e.** The chef's potatoes
   **f.** Brick's weights

## Page 44

**1 a.** It's   **b.** its   **c.** its   **d.** It's

**2 a.** It has been a long day.
   **b.** "It is only a ten-minute walk," she promised.

## Page 45

**1 a.** your    **b.** your    **c.** you're   **d.** You're
   **e.** your    **f.** you're   **g.** your    **h.** you're

## Pages 46-47

**1** april, bogart, tokyo

**2 a.** It all began on a dark and stormy night in December.
   **b.** Yin and Yang go bowling every Tuesday.
   **c.** "Bogart and I have a cunning plan," admitted Brick.

**d.** Plato dreams of opening a restaurant in Thailand.

**3 a.** The stormy weather made Armie's journey from France to Australia incredibly difficult.
   **b.** The weather by the lake house was at its best in the summer months, especially July and August.
   **c.** "I'm too hot!" admitted Plato after only five minutes in the sweltering hot sun.
   **d.** Brick realized that he hadn't showered since Monday ... four weeks ago.

## Page 48

**1 a.** ? **b.** . **c.** ? **d.** ? **e.** . **f.** ?

**2** How does the internet work?
Where is my left shoe?
When are we going to school?
Why is the sky blue?

**3 Your answers might include:**
   **a.** How old are you?
   **b.** What color are jellyfish?

## Page 49

**1 a.** .   **b.** !   **c.** .   **d.** !   **e.** ?   **f.** !

**2** Any answer relating to Armie's terrible smell and ending with an exclamation mark is correct.

## Pages 50-51

**1 a.** "I'd like to borrow this book please," said Armie.
   **b.** "That bee stung me!" cried Grit.
   **c.** "Why are carrots orange?" wondered Bearnice.
   **d.** "Now mix together all the ingredients," instructed Oz.

**2 a.** "Thank you," said Plato.
   **b.** "Where are you going?" asked Oz.
   **c.** "Stop that thief!" shouted Bogart.
   **d.** "See you tomorrow," said Yang.

## Pages 52-53

**1 a.** Mondays, Thursdays, and Fridays.
  **b.** German, Hindi, Welsh, Vietnamese, and English.
  **c.** tacos, burritos, burgers, and noodles.
  **d.** Switzerland, Australia, India, and Brazil.
  **e.** Monday, Tuesday, Wednesday, Thursday, Friday, Saturday, and Sunday.

**2** Any answer that is a full sentence, includes a list of fruits separated by commas, and ends with a period is correct.

**3 a.** strawberry ripple, cookie dough, and chocolate chip.
  **b.** a new laptop, green sneakers, and a birthday cake.
  **c.** clean the living room, dust the shelves, and wash the dishes.
  **d.** the raspberry cupcake, the cinnamon swirl, the jelly doughnut, and the hazelnut macaron.

## Pages 54-55

**1 a.** True  **b.** False  **c.** False  **d.** True

**2** It was a quiet, peaceful place. // The other trolls did not understand Steve's constant dancing.

## Pages 56-57

**1 a.** Other reptiles include crocodiles and turtles.
  **b.** Things will start to brighten up on Friday.
  **c.** Jewelry can be very expensive.
  **d.** The capital city is Kuala Lumpur, and the official language is Malay.

**2** Planet Earth has one moon. // Jupiter is the largest planet in the solar system. Scientists think that Jupiter has 79 moons. // Mercury is the closest planet to the sun and one of the closest planets to Earth.

**3** Any answer that includes two paragraphs of three full sentences is correct.

## Pages 58-59

**1 Puddles:** Small pools of water ...
  **Oceans:** Huge expanses of saltwater ...
  **Rivers:** Large natural streams of water ...

**2 Your answers might include:**
  **a.** Mars  **b.** The Sun  **c.** Moons

## Pages 62-63

**1 a.** happy, ecstatic
  **b.** sad, glum
  **c.** miserable, melancholy
  **d.** delighted, thrilled
  **e.** sorrowful, gloomy

**2** Any suitable replacement for happy or sad is correct.

## Pages 64-65

| **1** | a. 5 | b. 5 | c. 2 | d. 1 | e. 3 |
|---|---|---|---|---|---|
| | f. 2 | g. 3 | h. 5 | i. 4 | j. 2 |
| | k. 3 | l. 4 | m. 2 | n. 1 | o. 3 |
| | p. 4 | q. 1 | r. 1 | s. 5 | t. 4 |

## Pages 66-67

**1 a.** jellyfish    **b.** sunflower
  **c.** butterfly    **d.** rainbow
  **e.** paintbrush

**2** Any full sentences using the words **pancake**, **cowboy**, **afternoon**, or **football** are correct.

## Pages 68-69

**1** usual, unusual, usually
  behave, misbehave, behavior
  alone, lonely, lonesome
  friend, unfriendly, friendship
  myself, itself, yourself
  agree, agreement, disagree
  play, playful, replay
  sad, sadly, sadness

**Pages 70-75**

1  a.   b.   c.   d.

   e.   f.   g.   h.

   i.   j.

2  **a.** reign  **b.** rain  **c.** reign
   **d.** rain  **e.** rain  **f.** rain

3  **a.** meat  **b.** weather  **c.** berry
   **d.** fare  **e.** grate  **f.** mane
   **g.** medal  **h.** mist

4  **a.** eight  **b.** great  **c.** bury
   **d.** whether  **e.** meet

**Pages 76-77**

1  **a.** chest  **b.** tap  **c.** lie  **d.** foot

2  a.   b.   c.

   d.   e.           f.

**Pages 78-79**

1  **a.** Brick  **b.** Yang  **c.** Bearnice
   **d.** Bogart  **e.** Brick  **f.** Plato

**Pages 80-81**

1  **a.** submerged  **b.** superpowers
   **c.** supermarket  **d.** superstars
   **e.** subzero

**Pages 82-83**

1  **a.** untidy  **b.** misbehave  **c.** disbelief
   **d.** unwell  **e.** dislikes

**Page 85**

1  **Synonyms:** thick, heavy, solid
   **Word pairs:** forest, book, fog
   **Sentence example:** The explorer could barely see through the dense fog.

2  **Synonyms:** cloudy, misty, foggy
   **Word pairs:** sky, memories, sunshine
   **Sentence example:** Armie squinted at the hazy cloud above him.

**Page 86**

1  **Synonyms:** boring, plain, tasteless
   **Word pairs:** statement, food, colors
   **Sentence example:** The bland sandwich needed a lot of extra seasoning.

2  **Synonyms:** sharp, zesty, sour
   **Word pairs:** fruit, sauce, jelly
   **Sentence example:** Shang High's eyes watered as he tasted the tangy grapefruit.

**Page 87**

1  **Synonyms:** see, spot, notice
   **Word pairs:** briefly, suddenly, unexpectedly
   **Sentence example:** Yin glimpsed a small mouse hiding behind the picnic basket.

2  **Synonyms:** peek, gaze, stare
   **Word pairs:** down, curiously, inside
   **Sentence example:** Bogart peered over his shoulder suspiciously.

**Pages 90-93**

1  **a.** snail
   **b.** plane, wait
   **c.** Today, sailed, lake

2  **a.** sheep, valley
   **b.** monkey, meal
   **c.** chief, thief

3  **a.** invite, July
   **b.** might, tonight
   **c.** why, lie

4  **a.** phone, coat  **b.** yellow, goal
   **c.** toad, home  **d.** snowy, slope

5  **a.** room, broom  **b.** tissue
   **c.** tooth, grew  **d.** choose, flute

## Pages 94-95

**1 a.** burn   **b.** thirsty   **c.** purple
**d.** herbs   **e.** weather  **f.** world

**2** weather, weather, world, birthday,
burger, circus, surfing, purple, Thursday

## Page 96

**1 a.** jaw       **b.** call      **c.** small
**d.** claw     **e.** ball      **f.** dawn
**g.** chalkboard  **h.** hawk    **i.** wall
**j.** walk

## Page 97

**1** knight, knocked, gnome, wrinkly,
writes, knight, knitting, knees, wriggle,
designed, gnome, sign, Knight, knight,
gnome

## Pages 98-99

**1 a. sh**ark  **b. s**ure **c.** ma**ch**ine  **d.** i**ss**ue

**2 sh: sh**out, vani**sh**
**s: s**ure, **s**ugar
**ch:** para**ch**ute, ma**ch**ine
**ss:** ti**ss**ue, i**ss**ue

**3 a.** vanished   **b.** parachute
**c.** machine   **d.** sugar

## Page 100

**1** orange, genius, angel

**2 a.** engine   **b.** stage   **c.** original
**d.** jungle   **e.** gymnast  **f.** jacket
**g.** giant, bridge

## Page 101

**1 ci**r**c**le: the first c is soft,
the second c is hard

**2** center, century, certain

**3 a.** castle **b.** voice  **c.** celery **d.** mice

## Pages 102-103

**1 a.** waved   **b.** slipped   **c.** worried
**d.** asked   **e.** cried   **f.** dropped

**2 a.** slamming  **b.** writing  **c.** stepping

**d.** closing   **e.** watching   **f.** nodding

## Pages 104-105

**1 a.** friendlier   **b.** safer
**c.** rarer        **d.** fitter

**2 a.** strangest   **b.** scariest
**c.** luckiest    **d.** hottest

## Pages 106-107

**1 a.** shelves  **b.** butterflies  **c.** wolves
**d.** benches **e.** houses     **f.** bushes
**g.** elves    **h.** trophies

**2 a.** thieves  **b.** strawberries  **c.** wishes
**d.** dishes   **e.** bunnies     **f.** loaves

## Pages 108-109

**1** man > men        die > dice
woman > women   fish > fish
tooth > teeth      person > people
fungus > fungi    goose > geese
ox > oxen        deer > deer
child > children   mouse > mice

## Pages 110-111

**1 a.** beautiful     **b.** happiness
**c.** hopeless    **d.** painful
**e.** enjoyment   **f.** loneliness
**g.** merciful     **h.** greediness

**2 a.** silliness   **b.** pitiful   **c.** windiness
**d.** penniless  **e.** improvement

## Page 112

**1 a.** teacher    **b.** gardener
**c.** builder     **d.** cleaner
**e.** player      **f.** photographer
**g.** writer      **h.** farmer

## Page 113

**1 a.** innocently   **b.** humbly
**c.** generously   **d.** sarcastically
**e.** ferociously

## Pages 114-115

**1 a.** information   **b.** expectation
**c.** publication

**2 a.** accusation    **b.** admiration
   **c.** invitation

**3 a.** location   **b.** donation    **c.** education

**4** information, examination, expectation, location, education

## Pages 116-117

**1 a.** joyous         **b.** mountainous
   **c.** villainous

**2 a.** adventurous   **b.** nervous
   **c.** ridiculous

**3 a.** odorous       **b.** poisonous
   **c.** carnivorous

**4 a.** ridiculous      **b.** villainous
   **c.** adventurous   **d.** nervous

## Pages 118-119

**1 a.** measure    **b.** creature    **c.** pleasure
   **d.** furniture     **e.** adventure   **f.** picture

**2 a.** picture      **b.** creature
   **c.** measure    **d.** pleasure
   **e.** furniture     **f.** adventure

## Pages 120-121

**1 a.** business     **b. eigh**t     **c.** February
   **d. i**s**l**and      **e.** fam**ous**    **f.** len**g**th
   **g. n**a**ugh**ty     **h. h**e**igh**t

**2 a.** height     **b.** famous    **c.** island
   **d.** eight      **e.** length     **f.** February
   **g.** naughty    **h.** business

## Pages 124-129

**1** b, c

**2** b

**3 Your answer might be something like:**
"The farmer goes home and leaves the orchard unguarded."

**4** b

**5 a.** 2    **b.** 4    **c.** 1    **d.** 3

**6 Your answer might be something like:**
"Embarrassed," "Angry," or "Frustrated"

**7 Your answer might be something like:**
"He couldn't reach them." or
"He wants to pretend that he didn't want them."

## Pages 130-133

**1** b

**2** $947 million

**3** Berlin, Madrid, Paris

**4** c

**5 Your answer might be something like:**
"People disagree about whether esports should be counted as sports."

**6 a. Your answer might be:**
   "It talks about how esports are becoming more popular every year."
   **b. Your answer might be:**
   "The Esports Controversy" or
   "Is it a sport?"

**7** Any answer that uses full sentences to argue a point of view is correct.

## Pages 134-139

**1 a.** false    **b.** true    **c.** true    **d.** false
   **e.** true    **f.** false

**2** b

**3** farmer, baker, priest, doctor, merchant

**4** because the soil was fertile

**5** a, c

**6** a

**7 Your answer might be something like:**
"a pet," "a necklace," or "gold."

**8 a. and** it was also used to transport things by boat.
   **b. but** they did eat fish.
   **c. but** those who could write used hieroglyphs.
   **d. or** they might go to work as a baker.
   **e. and** they worshiped over 2,000 gods and goddesses.

## Pages 140-149

1 a gardening podcast

2 **a.** false   **b.** false   **c.** true

3 **a.** resolution   **b.** climax
  **c.** opening   **d.** build-up

4 **Your answer might be something like:**
  "relieved," "confused," or "pleased"

5 They love each other.

6 **a.** Brick's gym socks
  **b.** a pungent old cheese and anchovy
    sandwich
  **c.** as abrasive as nails on a chalkboard

7 Yin's voice was grating and unpleasant.
  Yin says that Yang smells strongly.

8 **Your answers might be something like:**
  **a.** rumbling thunder   **b.** statue
  **c.** rotten eggs   **d.** a dump

## Pages 150-155

1 **a.** 5   **b.** 1   **c.** 2   **d.** 3   **e.** 4

2 **Your answer might be something like:**
  "The experiment is too messy to do
  indoors!"

3 hair dryer, recipe book, black pepper

4 22,615 feet (6,893 meters) tall

5 **a.** Cut   **b.** Wait   **c.** mix

6 **Your answer might be something like:**
  "Erupt means to explode."

7 **Your answer might be something like:**
  "A real volcano would be too big and
  too dangerous."

8 to instruct

9 **Your answer might be something like:**
  "Put toothpaste on your toothbrush.
  Brush your teeth gently.
  Spit out the extra toothpaste.
  Rinse your toothbrush and put it away."

## Pages 156-163

1 **Your answer might be something like:**
  "The poem is about a world where
  everything is the opposite of what it
  normally is."

2 **Your answer might be something like:**
  "Opposite Land" or "A Surprising Fall"

3 grumpy, sighed, scowled

4 **Your answer might be something like:**
  "He fell over." or "He slipped."

5 **Your answer might be something like:**
  "He feels scared." or "He feels surprised."

6 bump

7 He tastes salt.

8 Fish don't swim on land!

9 a, d, e

10 Armie: audacious   Oz: shy
   Bearnice: graceful   Brick: weak

11 "Even his friends seemed a little
   bit odd"

12 **Your answer might be something like:**
   "Sugar was salty and salt was sweet.
   Broccoli was orange. Hands were feet."

## Pages 170-171

1 Shang Highs > Shang High's
  on? cried > on?" cried
  whether > weather
  had'nt > hadn't
  an orange a pepper an apple an
  apricot and a lot of cabbages > an
  orange, a pepper, an apple, an apricot,
  and a lot of cabbages
  a alarming rate > an alarming rate
  an fallen apple > a fallen apple

2 **Your answer might be something like:**
  "Suddenly, a watermelon crashed
  loudly into the roof of a car."

# COOKED UP BY MRS WORDSMITH'S CREATIVE TEAM

**Pedagogy Lead**
Eleni Savva

**Writers**
Tatiana Barnes
Amelia Mehra

**Academic Advisor**
Emma Madden

**Creative Director**
Lady San Pedro

**Designers**
Holly Jones
Jess Macadam
Evelyn Wandernoth
James Webb

**Lead Designer**
James Sales

**Producer**
Leon Welters

**Artists**
Brett Coulson
Phil Mamuyac
Aghnia Mardiyah
Nicolò Mereu
Daniel J. Permutt

**With characters by**
Craig Kellman

## No animals were harmed in the making of these illustrations.

**Project Managers**
**Senior Editor** Helen Murray
**US Editor** Kayla Dugger
**Senior Designer** Anna Formanek
**Project Editor** Lisa Stock

**Senior Production Editor** Jennifer Murray
**Senior Production Controllers** Louise Minihane
and Mary Slater
**Publishing Director** Mark Searle

First American Edition, 2022
Published in the United States by DK Publishing
1450 Broadway, Suite 801, New York, NY 10018

Printed and bound in Malaysia

For the curious

**www.dk.com**

mrswordsmith.com

This book was made with
Forest Stewardship Council™
certified paper – one small
step in DK's commitment to
a sustainable future.

**The building blocks of reading**

READ TO LEARN

LEARN TO READ

| Phonemic Awareness | Phonics | Fluency | Vocabulary | Reading Comprehension |

**Readiculous App**
App Store & Google Play

**Word Tag App**
App Store & Google Play

# OUR JOB IS TO INCREASE YOUR CHILD'S READING AGE

This book adheres to the science of reading. Our research-backed learning helps children progress through phonemic awareness, phonics, fluency, vocabulary, and reading comprehension.